LAKE TAHOE

HOW TO USE THIS GUIDEBOOK

This guidebook is divided into four sections: *An Introduction to Lake Tahoe*, *The History of Lake Tahoe*, *South Lake Tahoe*, and *North Lake Tahoe*.

The first two sections comprise essays, designed to provide you with facts on the area.

In the next two sections we explore the Lake Tahoe Basin, with a detailed, geographical breakdown of the area. Each section contains descriptions of the various places and points of interest, followed by a sub-section entitled *Practical Information*. The *Practical Information* is designed to provide you with a ready reference to accommodations, restaurants, tours, places of interest, recreation areas, transportation, etc., with addresses and phone numbers.

A quick and easy way into this book is the *Index* at the end.

Titles in this Series

The Complete Gold Country Guidebook
The Complete Lake Tahoe Guidebook
The Complete Monterey Peninsula Guidebook
The Complete San Diego Guidebook
The Complete San Francisco Guidebook
The Complete Santa Barbara Guidebook
The Complete Wine Country Guidebook
Farm Tours of Northern California
Vacation Towns of California

Indian Chief Travel Guides are available from your local bookstore or Indian Chief Publishing House, P.O. Box 5205, Tahoe City, CA 95730.

The Complete
LAKE TAHOE
Guidebook

Published by Indian Chief Publishing House
Tahoe City, California

Area Editor: **B. SANGWAN**
Editorial Associate: **PHILLIPPA J. SAVAGE**
Photographs : **Heavenly Valley Ski Resort,**
    Northstar-at-Tahoe, M.S. Dixie Cruises,
    Royal Gorge/David Madison,
    Ron Gramanz, B. Sangwan

ISBN 0-916841-15-4

Printed in the U.S.A.

CONTENTS

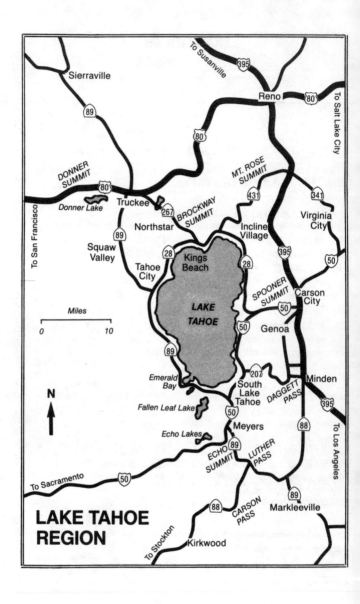

LAKE TAHOE
REGION

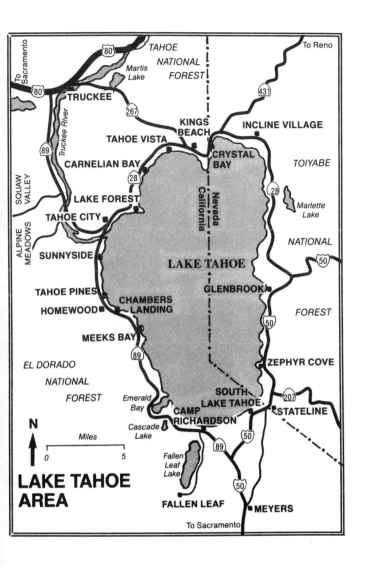

LAKE TAHOE AREA

AN INTRODUCTION TO LAKE TAHOE

A Destination Resort

Lake Tahoe is one of the most beautiful lakes in the world, and the largest among North America's alpine lakes (second largest in the world). Mark Twain once wrote of it: "A noble sheet of blue water lifted six thousand three hundred feet above the level of the sea, and walled in by a rim of snow clad mountain peaks ... as it lay there with the shadows of the mountains brilliantly photographed upon its still surface, I thought it must surely be the fairest picture the whole earth affords."

Lake Tahoe is situated at an elevation of 6229 feet, more or less in the center of the Sierra Nevada mountain range, with a third of it lying in the State of Nevada and two-thirds in California. From San Francisco the lake is 193 miles distant, and from Reno, Nevada, 54 miles. The lake itself is 22 miles long and 12 miles wide, with a maximum depth of 1645 feet. It is fed by 63 different feeder creeks, streams and rivers, and has a water capacity of 122,160,280 acre-feet (nearly four times that of Lake Mead, the largest man-made lake in the world). Its shoreline measures 71 miles, 42 miles of which lie in California. The Lake Tahoe Basin comprises about 480 square miles (an area larger than Rhode Island), made up mostly of lush, evergreen forests and sculpted granite mountains.

Nearly 11 million people visit the Lake Tahoe (and Reno) area every year, and most come back a second time. There are approximately

10,000 motel rooms and over 200 restaurants to be found in the Tahoe area alone, with hundreds of thousands of acres of preserved wilderness and a vast array of year-round recreational facilities, including fishing, boating, swimming, wind-surfing, hiking, rock-climbing, horseback riding, golf, bicycling and skiing. Lake Tahoe also boasts one of the finest casino districts in the country, with Las Vegas-style casinos, and has the largest concentration of ski areas in the world—some 20 different ski resorts, with a total of nearly 160 mechanical ski lifts. And to add to this, Lake Tahoe enjoys four distinct seasons: spring, summer, fall and winter. Average snowfall in the region is 300 inches, and yet there are some 250 clear, sunny days every year.

Indeed, Lake Tahoe is among the choicest destination resorts in the world.

THE HISTORY OF
LAKE TAHOE

Lake Tahoe began forming nearly 25 million years ago when portions of the upthrust that comprised the Sierra Nevada mountain range experienced a vast disturbance, causing it to crack and leave a twin, serrated crest and a trough-like depression. More than 20 million years later came the volcanic age, during which huge quantities of lava poured into the trough, pushing masses of boulder ahead of it to form a lateral ridge damming up the southern half of the trough. Then, eight or nine thousand years ago, a massive glacier originating in the south moved northward through the region. This was known as the Lake Valley glacier. Several feeder glaciers from it gouged out the surrounding smaller troughs and valleys. Three fine examples of these are Fallen Leaf Lake, Cascade Lake and Emerald Bay; the Emerald Bay glacier pack actually extended into the oval of Lake Tahoe and later joined the main body of ice. When the ice finally melted, the waters rose several hundred feet above the present level of the lake and forged an outlet in the northwest, through what is now the Truckee River Canyon; although a disputed theory maintains that the Truckee River Canyon was formed by an off-shoot glacier, while the main body of ice moved northeast into Nevada's desert valleys.

Another less likely version of the formation of Lake Tahoe is offered in an ancient Indian legend, which suggests that Lake Tahoe and all the other smaller lakes and ponds in the region were formed by the mythical "Water Babies," small gray creatures with long dark hair, who have the power to flood the world. It is told that once the Damalalii, a short-tailed weascl, scalped a water baby, and the water baby became angry and flooded the entire region, forcing the Damalalii to return the scalp, lest he drown in the high, rising waters. After the return of the scalp, the waters receded to their present level. And thus was formed Lake Tahoe.

The first known inhabitants of the Lake Tahoe Basin were the Washoe Indians, a mobile people from the arid country east of the Sierra. The Washoe were primarily gatherers, with seeds and pinyon nuts comprising their staple diet. In summer they made camp at Lake Tahoe, and fished in its waters. They called the lake "Tahoe," meaning "big water in high place." Others inhabiting the area were the Paiute Indians, who remained largely in the southern parts of the basin. Three larger Indian tribes dwelled in the western foothills of the Sierra, though they never extended their range to Tahoe.

White man first sighted the Sierra Nevada mountain range in 1776: a Franciscan missionary named Pedro Font, member of the Anza expedition, stood on a hill near the mouth of the Sacramento River to behold what he later described as *"un gran sierra nevada,"* meaning "a great snow-covered mountain range." But Lake Tahoe was not discovered until nearly seventy years later, on February 14, 1844. The discovery was made by the Fremont Party, led by Captain John Charles Fremont of the U.S. Topographical Engineers, and including Kit Carson, the famous scout, and a German topographer named Charles Preuss. The party was on the eastern ridges of the Sierra, in search of a pass leading from the Carson Valley to the Valley of the Sacramento, when Fremont and Preuss went on ahead to take observations. They ascended what is now known as Red Lake Peak, and saw before them, some 15 miles distant, a vast blue lake, so completely surrounded by mountains that, as Fremont later wrote, they "could not discover an outlet." Fremont named the lake "Bonpland," after the eminent French botanist, Aime Jacques Alexandre Bonpland, who accompanied Barron von Humboldt to explore the West. Preuss made mention of it as the "Mountain Lake." In 1852, however, the lake was named "Bigler," in honor of the Governor of Califoria, John Bigler, who led a rescue party to the aid of a group of emigrants snowbound in Lake Valley that year. But the governor soon fell into disfavor due to his Confederate leanings during the Civil War, and the lake was renamed in 1861. The lake was then called "Tahoe," after much debate over the precise meaning of the word.

The 1840's, after the discovery, were a period of trailblazing. Several emigrant parties searched for passes over the Sierra range in their attempts to reach the West. The Donner Party is well remembered as part of the region's history. In the winter of 1846-47 the emigrant party led by George Donner became trapped in the treacherous snows near the Donner Pass. They camped just east of the pass, some by the Donner Lake. But the Donner families were ill-prepared for the bitter conditions they encountered, and food soon ran out. Hunger and cold gripped the camp. Several members of the party perished, while the survivors resorted to cannibalism to stay alive until they were found by a rescue party the following spring. Of a party of 89, 42 perished.

With the discovery of gold in 1848, a fresh wave of emigrants and gold seekers swarmed over the Sierra mountains. Several passes were opened up: Lassen, Beckwourth, Carson and Donner. The most traveled route, however, remained by way of Truckee, along which the railroad and Interstate 80 now pass.

In 1851 Lake Tahoe received its first white settler, Martin Smith, who established a trading post in the area known as Meyers now. Others soon followed. A trail was cut through Lake Valley (South Lake Tahoe) the following year by John Calhoun "Cockeye" Johnson, a Sierra pioneer, and appropriately named the Johnson Pass Cut-Off. The route followed roughly the path of present day Highway 50 from Placerville to Lake Valley, descending nearby the Meyers Grade into the valley; then circling around the southern parts of the lake and up along the southeast corner, it passed over the Spooner Summit and into the Carson Valley. In 1896 this became California's first state highway.

The Tahoe basin was mostly wilderness country during the early years, largely inaccessible. But in 1859, the discovery of the Comstock Lode, the richest silver deposit known to history, brought waves of miners and prospectors through Lake Valley enroute to the Washoe mines. In a matter of months the road from Placerville to Carson (City), via Lake Valley, which was essentially the Johnson Pass Cut-off route, became the most traveled in the continent. For nearly a decade wagon trains rolled along this narrow, dusty, rutted trail, almost ceaselessly. In 1860, some 400 wagons traveled this road daily, and more than $1,350,000 was collected in tolls alone. By 1862 the passenger traffic on the road had soared to a staggering 56,500. Over 100 waystations, hotels and saloons sprouted between Placerville and Carson City, along what by then had come to be known as the Great Bonanza Road to Washoe, with at least a score and some dotting the Lake Valley section of the road. It is told that many of the waystations collected upwards of $1,000 in tolls in the course of a day, while some of the better saloons raked in as much as $3,000 in a single night. Such were the Bonanza days, a memorable chapter in Lake Valley's past.

Meanwhile, a transcontinental railroad was in the making, largely an endeavor of the Big Four: Charles Crocker, Collis P. Huntington, Mark Hopkins, and Leland Stanford, the Governor of California. Laying of the rails over the Sierra was the hardest part of it. Fifteen tunnels had to be blasted through the granite mountains, and more than 40 miles of track had to be put under cover, building "snow-sheds," to ward off the snow drifts that had hampered work on the tracks. More than 10,000 Chinese were brought in from San Francisco to provide the labor, and a railroad town, now known as Truckee, grew around the work force, just east of the Donner Pass. In April, 1868, the first train crossed the Sierra, eastbound. And the traffic through Lake Valley was diverted to over the Donner Pass.

By the late 1860's silver mining was progressing at a hectic pace just east of the Sierras, with new claims being made and new mines being built, and a burgeoning metropolis growing around it all. This, however, created a new demand: lumber. And Lake Tahoe's virgin forests provided a ready and seemingly inexhaustible source. A half dozen or so logging companies sprouted along the lake's east and south shores. The first shoreline sawmill had been built at Glenbrook in 1861, and now many others began sprouting along the lake's sides. In 1873 the Carson and Tahoe Lumber and Fluming Company was formed by Henry Marvin Yerington and Duane LeRoy Bliss, with Bliss as its president. In the following years the company acquired leases to several thousand acres of timberland, and spawned a vast network of sawmills, flumes, log-chutes, receiving ponds, tug boats, cordwood barges, and even a stretch of railroad employed in the transportation of logs. The company's operations were centered at Glenbrook, on the east shore. But by 1895 the timberlands on the Nevada side were largely depleted; the company had stripped nearly 50,000 acres of forest, leaving behind a scant 950 acres of useable stands of timber, and the operations were then moved to the California side. In its 28 years of operation, the C.& T. L.& F. Company took as much as 750,000,000 board feet of lumber and 500,000 cords of wood from the Lake Tahoe basin.

The late 1890's and early 1900's were good times for Lake Tahoe. Hundreds of summer vacationers thronged the lake's shores, led by social sets from San Francisco and Carson City. The over-water spur tracks and shoreline sawmills of the lumbering days gave way to fastidious over-water clubhouses and luxuriously appointed hostelries. The legendary three and one-half story hotel, The Tallac, billed as "the Saratoga of the Pacific," was built in 1898 on the southwestern shore of the lake. It catered to the well-heeled crowds of the day, providing guests with some of the finest cuisines in the continent, and an array of recreational activities, everything from plain promenading on the pebble beaches to back-packing, horseback riding, swimming, tennis, racquetball and fishing (specially trained guides took guests in fishing boats to the fishing "hot spots" of the lake, practically guaranteeing a catch); and even illegal gambling flourished. The price for lodging alone at The Tallac was $35.00 per week, and up. In 1901, a new "Saratoga," the Tahoe Tavern, was built just south of Tahoe City, and at about the same time a narrow-gauge railroad was pushed through the Truckee River Canyon, from Tahoe City to Truckee, where it linked up with the Southern Pacific railroad.

By the turn of the century the tug boats and cordwood barges of the lumbering days were gone from the scene too, replaced by luxury steam boats and pleasure vessels, and flotillas of holiday fishing boats. In 1896, the legendary *Tahoe* was launched, a 169-foot, 200-passenger steamer, which ruled the Lake Tahoe waters for some 44 years, until on August 29, 1940, it was scuttled just off the east shore.

The "Roaring 20's" ushered in yet another glorious era, with a host of rambling summer homes appearing quite randomly along the shoreline, among them the fabled "Vikingsholm," the "Thunderbird Lodge," the "Kellogg Mansion," the Pope and Tevis homes at the Tallac Estates, and "Fleur du Lac," industrialist Henry J. Kaiser's vacation home, on the west shore. The 1920's also witnessed the opening up of Tahoe to winter recreation. In fact, winter vacationing at the lake was so popular that in 1926 Southern Pacific introduced its "Snowball" specials to railroad eager tourists from San Francisco to Truckee, and from Truckee to Tahoe City. Just south of Tahoe City, near the Tahoe Tavern, an "Olympic Hill" (comprising a ski jump and a toboggan run) opened up at what became Lake Tahoe's first ski resort—

Granlibakken.

In the 1940's, right after World War II, a "casino district" began developing on the south shore, with a handful of casino-clubs cluttering the Nevada side of the stateline. The newly built highway system made travel to Tahoe easier, and the casinos flourished. In 1955, big name entertainment was introduced in Tahoe, mainly the effort of gaming pioneers Eddie Sahati and Harvey Gross, and in 1960 Lake Tahoe's first highrise appeared at the stateline: the 11-story, 200-room Harvey's Resort Hotel.

The year 1960 also brought the VIII Winter Olympic Games to Squaw Valley, 4 miles north of Tahoe City. The games are memorable for one event: the U.S. Hockey Team defeated the Russians 3-2, then went on to defeat Czechoslovakia 9-4 in the finals to win the gold medal. Not until 20 years later, in 1980 at Lake Placid, was the feat repeated.

For the next decade, Lake Tahoe experienced a real estate boom. Property prices soared and hundreds of summer homes sprouted throughout the basin. Large scale development began in the mid-1960's, with condominium complexes appearing along the shore-line. Concern was voiced over the unabated development and the resulting soil erosion, and the impact of it all on the clarity of the lake. The League to Save Lake Tahoe was formed in 1965, comprising mainly wealthy, influential lakers. And in 1969, a bi-state body, the Tahoe Regional Planning Agency, was created, solely for the purpose of controlling and regulating development in the Tahoe basin. New construction in the basin has been severely limited since, and more than 85% of Tahoe's land is now either state or federally owned, creating a bonanza of National Forests and State Parks.

In April of 1982, Lake Tahoe became the focus of the nation. An avalanche at Alpine Meadows leveled the ski lodge and several homes, claiming the lives of seven people. A young ski patrol member, Anna Conrad, miraculously survived the avalanche, buried beneath tons of snow for six whole days and nights.

Once again, in March, 1985, a world event came to Tahoe. Heavenly Valley hosted the prestigious World Cup skiing, and Lake Tahoe was briefly at the center of attention.

Lake Tahoe is today among the choicest destination resorts in the world. But a problem facing it is that of future growth. What direction should this take? How much building should be permitted? What would the environmental impact of it be on the lake? These are questions likely to linger for many years ahead.

SOUTH LAKE TAHOE

Tahoe's Big Apple

South Lake Tahoe, by Tahoe standards, is a bustling, thriving metropolis, where more than half of the Tahoe Basin's population lives; roughly 25,000 people. This is also a place that has been largely built around the tourist, with a cluster of highrise hotel-casinos at one end of it, and a preserved wilderness at the other. At the center of it lies a lively urban sprawl, concentrated with motels, shops and restaurants—nearly 9000 motel rooms within a space of some 10 square miles, and over 100 restaurants.

The greater South Lake Tahoe comprises broadly five sections: the City of South Lake Tahoe, the Stateline, the Southeast Corner, the Emerald Bay Route area, and the Bonanza Route area. The city is the largest and most central part. To its east lies the (California-Nevada) Stateline, home to South Tahoe's vibrant "casino district," and to its northwest is the Emerald Bay Route, an area of exceptional scenic beauty. South of the city is the historic Bonanza Route, which forms part of the original Great Bonanza Road, path of the "silver seekers" of the 1860's. And the Southeast Corner is the section to the east of the Stateline, comprising eight or nine miles of the southeastern shoreline, and the Kingsbury Grade to the south of there.

South Lake Tahoe can be reached by way of any of three state highways: 50, 89 or (Nevada Route) 207. The Lake Tahoe Airport, Lake Tahoe's only commercial airport, lies just to the south of the city area.

THE BONANZA ROUTE

Highway 50 west is the oldest and most traveled route leading into South Lake Tahoe, having first opened to wagon traffic in the 1850's. From Placerville it winds through several miles of mountain country, through Pollock Pines, Kyburz and Strawberry, following the South Fork of the American River for the most part, then loops over Echo Summit and resolutely descends into Lake Valley (South Lake Tahoe) at the twin divide of the Sierra Nevada-Carson Range. At the foot of the grade, known as the Meyers Grade, one encounters a vast, open meadow in the midst of which sits the township of Meyers, Lake Valley's oldest settlement and now the "gateway" to South Lake Tahoe. Beyond Meyers the highway continues almost directly north, while an historic back road, Pioneer Trail, branches to the northeast just past the township. Pioneer Trail is in fact the original Placerville-Carson back road, upon which much of the Bonanza traffic of the 1860's passed enroute to the Virginia City silver mines. The trail now skirts the City of South Lake Tahoe to the south and merges with the main thoroughfare, Lake Tahoe Boulevard (Highway 50), within two miles of the California-Nevada stateline, where stand South Tahoe's multi-storied hotel-casinos.

This, however, is the Great Bonanza Road, from Placerville to Virginia City, with Pioneer Trail and the Meyers area making up the Lake Tahoe segment of it.

Meyers

Meyers (also known as Tahoe Paradise) is a town of some importance, with a small number of shops and restaurants, two golf courses, a couple of schools, one or two campgrounds, and a rodeo ranch, Amaker's Ranch, which hosts South Tahoe's annual rodeo in summer. Meyers was first settled in 1851 by Martin Smith, Lake Valley's first white settler, though named later on for one George Henry Dudley Meyers, who owned much of the acreage here, from 1873 until practically the turn of the century. The site of Smith's original trading post, which in 1859 became Yank's Station, named for its illustrious new owner Ephraim "Yank" Clement, is to be seen on the east side of the highway, near the present day Yanks Station Resort; the site is marked by a Pony Express plaque, for Yank's in the 1860's, besides being the most colorful hostelry on the Bonanza Route, was also a remount station for Pony Express riders. Meyers, today, is also noted for its many hiking and nordic ski areas, a favorite among which is the Echo Lakes area, just two miles to the southwest, where a trail enchantingly journeys along the periphery of both the Upper and Lower Echo Lakes. In winter one may even find a snowmobiling meadow or two in the vicinity of the town, and a handful of ski rental shops along the highway. Worth visiting, too, are a couple of local restaurants, including the Freel Peak Saloon, a casual, inexpensive

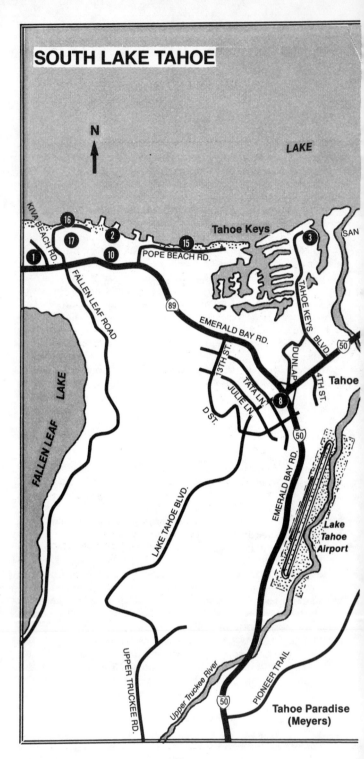

SOUTH LAKE TAHOE

N

LAKE

KIVA BEACH RD.

Tahoe Keys

SAN

16

17

2

15

3

1

10

POPE BEACH RD.

TAHOE KEYS BLVD.

FALLEN LEAF ROAD

89

EMERALD BAY RD.

DUNLAP

50

FALLEN LEAF LAKE

13TH ST.

TATA LN.

JULIE LN.

4TH ST.

Tahoe

8

D ST.

50

LAKE TAHOE BLVD.

EMERALD BAY RD.

Lake Tahoe Airport

UPPER TRUCKEE RD.

Upper Truckee River

PIONEER TRAIL

50

Tahoe Paradise (Meyers)

18

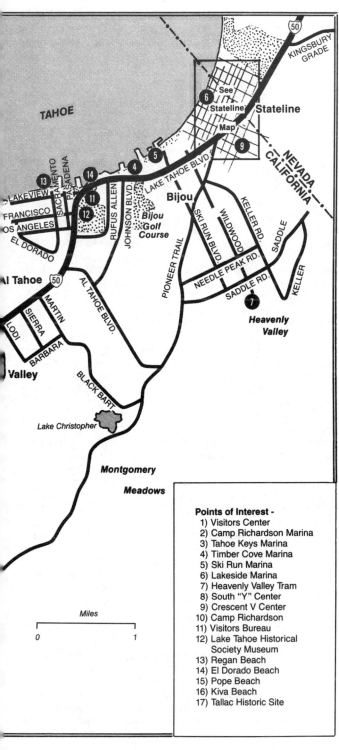

Points of Interest -
1) Visitors Center
2) Camp Richardson Marina
3) Tahoe Keys Marina
4) Timber Cove Marina
5) Ski Run Marina
6) Lakeside Marina
7) Heavenly Valley Tram
8) South "Y" Center
9) Crescent V Center
10) Camp Richardson
11) Visitors Bureau
12) Lake Tahoe Historical
   Society Museum
13) Regan Beach
14) El Dorado Beach
15) Pope Beach
16) Kiva Beach
17) Tallac Historic Site

diner, named for the mighty Freel Peak, the highest mountain at the lake with an elevation of 10,900 feet, seen farther to the east of here.

Pioneer Trail

Pioneer Trail is a lovely, tree-lined back road, some 7 miles long, frequently used as a city bypass route when traveling directly from Meyers to the Stateline. During the 1860's this was known as the "Placerville-Carson back road," for then, as now, the main road (the lakeshore road) ran farther to the north. The trail is noted mostly for its historic past, in particular the Bonanza era when it became one of the most traveled roads in the continent, with what has been described as "the greatest mass movement of men, wagons, materials, animals and bullion known to history," passing by way of it. A dozen or so waystations and hostelries were then located alongside of the trail, the sites of which have been marked with wooden pegs by the Lake Tahoe Historical Society, and can be visited; not all of these markers are readily visible though, with one or two of them really quite difficult to find, but it is nevertheless a worthwhile pursuit, especially for history buffs. (A guidebook worth taking along when exploring these sites is the Historical Society publication, *Lake Valley's Past*, which details an auto tour of these and other historical sites in the South Tahoe area, with numbered markers to go by.)

The site of Yank's Station, although in Meyers now, is considered to be the westernmost of the back road sites, with two others, the sites of the Celio Ranch and Osgood's Toll House, to be found farther southeast at the foot of the Meyers Grade. On the actual trail, however, proceeding northeast one first arrives at the site of Pine Grove House, located on the east side of the trail, one and one-half miles from Yank's. The Pine Grove House was built in 1860, expressly for the Bonanza trade, and by 1888 it was gone from the scene, gutted by fire. It had comprised one house and one barn.

One-half mile farther, on the same side of the road, is the site of Woodburn's Mill, where, in 1860, Robert Woodburn, a native of Ireland, built one of Lake Tahoe's earliest sawmills, the first ever to be powered by water. The 10-horsepower mill churned out a daily quota of 6000 board feet of double-width, out-size lumber, some of which is still to be seen in the sidewalls of some of Lake Valley's oldest homes. In its heyday, Woodburn's boasted a handful of logger's cabins, corrals for horses and cattle, a blacksmith's shop and even a post office. But by the late 1800's the lumbering settlement had all but vanished from the scene. One or two pieces of the mill machinery have been salvaged by the Lake Tahoe Historical Society and can be viewed at its museum on Lake Tahoe Boulevard.

At a pebble's throw from Woodburn's, where Trout Creek crosses beneath Pioneer Trail, there is a small bridge from the post-Bonanza era, believed to be the first such bridge constructed across the thorough-

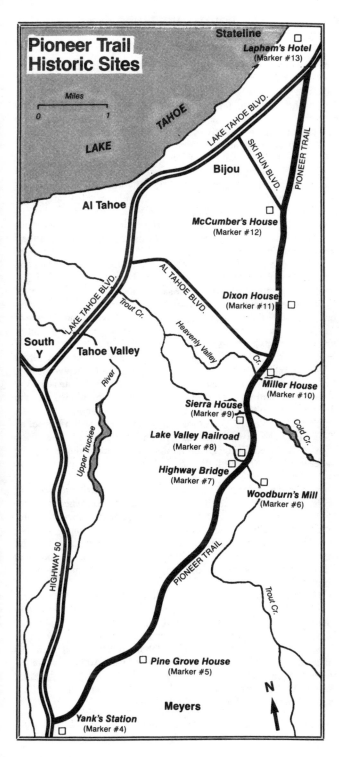

Pioneer Trail Historic Sites

Stateline
Lapham's Hotel (Marker #13)

Miles
0 — 1

LAKE TAHOE

Bijou

LAKE TAHOE BLVD.

SKI RUN BLVD.

PIONEER TRAIL

Al Tahoe

McCumber's House (Marker #12)

AL TAHOE BLVD.

Dixon House (Marker #11)

LAKE TAHOE BLVD.

Trout Cr.

Heavenly Valley

South Y

Tahoe Valley

River

Cr.

Miller House (Marker #10)

Sierra House (Marker #9)

Lake Valley Railroad (Marker #8)

Cold Cr.

Upper Truckee

Highway Bridge (Marker #7)

Woodburn's Mill (Marker #6)

PIONEER TRAIL

HIGHWAY 50

Trout Cr.

□ *Pine Grove House* (Marker #5)

N

Meyers

Yank's Station (Marker #4)

fare. The bridge is actually located just below the trail, on the west side of it. Above the bridge, just to the north of the creek, is the site of the Lake Valley Railroad tracks; it was along here that during the lumbering days of the 1880's the railroad passed. Impressions of the tracks had been visible for nearly one-half century after the dismantling of the railroad, but are now mostly overgrown with shrubs.

Beyond the bridge and the site of the railroad tracks, also on the west side of the trail, is the site of the most colorful of the back road hostelries: the Sierra House. A two-story log structure with an added saloon, the Sierra House was built in 1859 by Robert Garwood Dean, nephew of Judge Seneca Dean, who later went on to partake in the construction of the Lake Bigler House, the lake's first shoreline hostelry. Legend has it that Black Bart and Jack Bell, the notorious highway robbers, lodged at the Sierra House during the peak of their criminal activities, and that "Long Haired" Sam Brown—the coward killer from Washoe who carved 20 notches on the butt of his gun and maintained a private cemetary—as well as James Stewart, the "Silent Terror," frequented the Sierra House saloon. Later, even "The Whipped Murderess of Hangtown," notorious for poisoning her male companions, who was believed to have been whipped across her face by one of her victims, stayed a night here. By 1955, however, the Sierra House, not unlike other structures of the day, had been gutted by fire. Some of the lumber from the hostelry's outbuildings is now to be seen panelling one of the interior walls of the Sierra House School, located nearby.

A little over a mile to the northeast of the Sierra House site is the site of the Miller Station, a lesser known waystation, built in 1862 by John G. Miller to capitalize on the Washoe trade. And another half-mile from there, on the east side of the trail, is the site of Dixon House, an 80-feet-long and 38-feet-wide log structure, built in 1861. The Dixon House was named for the Dixon family, who owned and operated the hostelry from 1867 until it disappeared from the scene more than 50 years later.

Also on the east side of the road, approximately 200 yards south of Ski Run Boulevard, is the site of McCumber's House, where an early day laker named Freeman McCumber built a large two-story structure, with a domineering stone chimney and five outbuildings, in 1864. McCumber's was originally built as a primary residence but quickly fell prey to the Bonanza trade, and by the mid-1950's, it, too, had disappeared from the back road. The site has since been built upon with a private home.

The last site on the Placerville-Carson back road, located more or less on the "back road Y," is that of Lapham's Hotel, variously known as Lapham's Landing, Stateline Hotel, Carney's Station, and Lakeside. Actually, quite like the site of Yank's Station, this site is no longer on Pioneer Trail, for the trail ends at Lake Tahoe Boulevard, and Lapham's lies north of the boulevard at the lake end of Park Avenue, where the present day Lakeside Marina is now located. Lapham's was named for William W. Lapham, who built and owned the hotel from 1860 until 1875, when it finally burned to the ground.

THE CITY

The City of South Lake Tahoe, incorporated in 1965, is Tahoe's only real city. It covers an area of approximately 26 square miles, taking in the subdivisions of Tahoe Valley, Tahoe Keys, Al Tahoe, Bijou and Lakeside. It is bounded on its east by the California-Nevada stateline and on its west by the El Dorado National Forest, with the world-renowned Heavenly Valley and the Montgomery Meadows to its south and some 6 miles of shoreline to be enjoyed along its north.

If you take Highway 50 directly into South Lake Tahoe, past Meyers and the Pioneer Trail turnoff, the first signs of city life to be encountered are at the South Tahoe Y, where Highways 50 and 89 intersect and where city traffic and traffic signals become a glaring reality. The "Y" more or less represents the western end of the city. From here Highway 50 travels in a northeasterly direction to the Al Tahoe shoreline, then dips slightly before heading directly east to the Stateline, from where it follows a northeasterly course again, past the Kingsbury Grade turnoff. The section of highway between the "Y" and the Kingsbury Grade turnoff is known as Lake Tahoe Boulevard. This is the city's main street, upon which much of the city's activity is centered, with scores of hotels, motels, timeshare condominiums, shops, restaurants and even some wedding chapels to be seen along here. The city also has an in-city campground, a golf course, a modest hospital, a couple of recreation areas, a visitors' information center, a museum and a Chamber of Commerce, all nestled along the boulevard. Most other urban and recreational facilities are to be found on four or five of the other major streets of the city, such as the Rufus Allen and Al Tahoe Boulevards, Park Avenue, Stateline Avenue and Ski Run Boulevard. Thus, in many ways, the city is really quite easy to explore, with little need to deviate from the major thoroughfares.

Tahoe Valley

Tahoe Valley is the westernmost section of the city, bordered on the west and northwest by the El Dorado National Forest and on the east by the Upper Truckee River. At the heart of the valley lies the South Tahoe Y (also known as the Tahoe Valley Y), crossroads of South Lake Tahoe for over a century, and now a vital business center of the valley. At the Y is to be found the South Y Center, one of South Tahoe's two biggest shopping centers, with two chain stores, a splendid bookstore, a movie theatre, and several small novelty stores and fast food outlets. A half-dozen or so smaller shopping squares are located nearby, within a two-mile radius of the Y. Just south of the Y are two campgrounds, and farther south of there the Lake Tahoe Airport, a typical mountain airport that dates from 1959. The airport, situated at an elevation of 6264 feet, boasts an 8544-foot north-south runway and a modest, shingled terminal building with an A-Frame facade, built in 1973. A half-mile or so south of the airport lies the Lake Tahoe Country Club, an 18-hole, 6588-yard golf course that also offers some exciting snowmobiling possibilities in winter.

North of the Y, on the Emerald Bay Road section of Highway 89 are a handful of rustic motels, interspersed with one or two excellent restaurants, notable among which are the Chez Villaret, a charming French restaurant, and Cantina Los Tres Hombres, which serves some delightful Mexican fare. During the summer months a couple of bicycle and moped rental outlets can be found along here too.

West of the Y lies a small, relatively quiet part of town, backed by the twin-peaked Tahoe Mountain (elevations 7249 and 7127 feet). Here are to be found a handful of residential tracts, a trailer park or two, and the City Administration and City Services centers, both located on Tata Lane.

To the east of the Y, and disected by Lake Tahoe Boulevard, lies South Lake Tahoe's bustling business district, where, some two miles or so along, one can visit the Swiss Chalet, an open-ended mall built in the European country tradition, with stucco walls, dark walnut trim and Tudor murals on the feature walls; there are some worthwhile variety stores and a delightful Swiss restaurant housed at the Chalet. A little farther, just past the intersection of Lake Tahoe Boulevard and Tahoe Keys Boulevard, and also of interest, is the Jewelry Factory, made famous by Sammy Davis, Jr. and the late Liberace, both of whom are said to have bought much of their jewelry here. Adjacent to the Jewelry Factory is The Outdoorsman, one of the best-known sporting goods stores at the lake, where one can buy everything from a hiking guidebook to fishing accessories, scuba diving outfits, ski equipment, bicycles, hunting knives and rifles. Not far from The Outdoorsman, the Upper Truckee River crosses beneath the highway as it heads for the lake; in spring it is possible to watch large schools of whitefish here, as they emerge from their spawning beds farther upstream.

Tahoe Keys

Almost directly north of Tahoe Valley lies Tahoe Keys, the smallest, newest, and most affluent section of the city. Tahoe Keys is made up of long narrow, lateral projections of land, with most of the homes here enjoying secluded waterfront settings. Of particular interest at Tahoe Keys is the Tahoe Keys Marina, located at the end of Venice Drive, which runs off Tahoe Keys Boulevard. It has on it, as its chief attraction, the Fresh Ketch, a delightful seafood restaurant. The marina also has some possibilities for boat charters.

Just west of Tahoe Keys lies the Truckee Marsh, characterized by scrub and brush and shallow water, and to the east the Upper Truckee River fans out into the lake.

Al Tahoe

Adjoining Tahoe Keys and Tahoe Valley on the east is Al Tahoe, a section of town that officially came into being in 1907 when a hotel of the same name was built here by one "Al" Sprague, who tacked on his "Al" to "Tahoe" to give the establishment a name. The original Al Tahoe subdivision, a triangular tract with a lake frontage, lies to the northwest of Lake Tahoe Boulevard, just where the boulevard swoops northeast to hug the shoreline. Several old homes and cottages, many of them dating from the 1920's, are to be found dotting the streets here. The site of the original Al Tahoe Hotel can be seen at the corner of Sacramento Street and Lakeview Avenue; upon it there now stands the Globin Home, a fire-brick building with a hand-hewn upper deck that looks out over the lake, originally built in 1924 as part of the old Globin Resort. Four or five well-aged cottages, part of the former Globin Resort, are scattered farther back on Sacramento Street. Just below the Globin Home lies Regan Beach, a lovely stretch of yellow sand, and at the edge of the subdivision, about one-half mile east of the influx of the Upper Truckee River into the lake, is to be seen the site of Lake House (also known as Lake Bigler House), the first of Lake Tahoe's shoreline hostelries, built in 1859 and gutted by fire in 1866.

Adjacent to the triangular Al Tahoe tract, on the east side of it, are the tiny El Dorado Recreation Area and a thin strip of beach of the same name, both wedged between the highway and the lake; the recreation area features a dozen or so park benches, all looking out over the lake. South of the recreation area, on the other side of the highway, lies the City Campground, with some 166 campsites, and beside the campground, in a park-like setting, is to be found a cluster of small brown buildings, housing the South Lake Tahoe Chamber of Commerce, the Lake Tahoe Arts Center and the Lake Tahoe Historical Society Museum. The museum is of particular interest; it has displays of old photographs depicting Lake Valley's past, as well as several interesting artifacts, a few of them of Indian origin. An out-sized bobsled, dating from the 1920's, can also be seen here, with some 19th century farm machinery on display just outside the museum building. Directly across the street from the complex sits the gray and white Tribune Building, home to the *Tahoe Daily Tribune*, Lake Tahoe's only daily newspaper.

The City Campground is flanked on its east by the Rufus Allen Boulevard, where one can visit the new City Library, with its many volumes of books providing for some literary interest. Nearby, roughly at the corner of Rufus Allen and the highway, is to be seen a weathered, dark-brown cabin, 40 feet square and propped on pilings. This is the Osgood Toll House, Tahoe's oldest structure, originally built in 1859 by one Nehemiah Osgood and located at the foot of the Meyers Grade. It was then a colorful Bonanza Route waystation, and also the site of an historic shootout between two highway robbers and the sheriff and his posse. The toll house was moved to its present location in the early 1970's.

Bijou

Bijou (meaning "gem" or "jewel") is the easternmost section of the city, named for a beautiful granite sand beach that once graced its shoreline, until in 1910 the damming of the lake's only outlet at Tahoe

City and the subsequent raising of the lake level devoured it completely. Bijou is the south shore's oldest business center, where in the 1880's and 1890's much of Lake Valley's large scale lumbering operations were centered. It has since grown into one of the most intensely developed sections of the city, with a wealth of fine shops, restaurants and motels, quite like any vibrant city center. Several sections of Bijou are well worth exploring on foot, quite at random really, with emphasis on the section between Ski Run Boulevard and Park Avenue, where the development is almost uninterrupted. There are a handful of exclusive timeshare condominium complexes to be found in the area as well, notable among them the Beach and Ski Club.

Bijou also has two delightful marinas, the Timber Cove Marina and the Ski Run Marina. Timber Cove is the older of the two, located just to the back of the Timber Cove Lodge, and not readily visible from the highway. It is noted for its 1000-foot pier, which is among the longest at the lake. Just to the west of the Timber Cove pier is the site of the ancient Bijou Pier, which is believed to have measured over 1800 feet, with the Lake Valley Railroad's narrow-gauge tracks running onto it, all the way to the far end; it was from here that Lake Valley's lumber was barged across the lake to the Glenbrook sawmills on the east shore during the lumbering days of the late 1800's. To the east of the Timber Cove Marina, situated at the foot of Ski Run Boulevard, is the Ski Run Marina, home port of the majestic *Tahoe Queen*, a 500-passenger, glass-bottomed cruise boat built in the Mississippi riverboat tradition, with a giant red paddlewheel mounted on its stern, white lace trim and rails along its open deck and passageways, and two great black chimneys rising above. The *Queen* cruises the lake waters year-round, featuring some worthwhile Emerald Bay Cruises, and Squaw Valley shuttles to the north shore in winter. South from the marina Ski Run Boulevard heads toward the world famous Heavenly Valley, with an array of ski rental shops to be seen dotting the roadsides enroute, interspersed with one or two hot-tub rental houses.

Also of interest at Bijou is the Bijou Golf Course, a 9-hole, 2015-yard course located between Fairway Avenue and Johnson Boulevard, just off the highway. This is the only in-city golf course, open to the public in summer.

To the east of Bijou lies Lakeside, a busy little section of town, with a marina, shopping district and several blocks of motels; and adjoining to the east of there, of course, is the California-Nevada Stateline.

STATELINE

The Stateline is one of the most vibrant parts of South Lake Tahoe and in many ways the hub of the area, with at least four different routes—Highway 50 west, Highway 50 east, the Kingsbury Grade (Nevada Route 207) and Pioneer Trail—converging in on it. On the Nevada side of it lies the celebrated "casino district" of South Tahoe, where stand some of the lake's finest hotel-casinos, and on the California side is to be found a profusion of motels and specialty shops, with most of these referring to their location as being "at the Stateline." And farther south from the casinos and motels lies Heavenly Valley, "America's largest alpine ski resort," part of it in Nevada and part in California.

Thus, in a rather broad, informal sort of way, the greater "Stateline" takes in the casino district, the small, ill-defined tract on the California side which theoretically belongs with the City of South Lake Tahoe, and, for practical purposes, even Heavenly Valley. (Although in a stricter sense the "Stateline" is only a small postal district on the Nevada side of the border).

The Casino District

Central to the Stateline is, of course, the casino district, a quarter-square-mile tract extending from the stateline east to Edgewood, along which are nestled a group of 24-hour casino-clubs and some of Tahoe's tallest buildings, fourteen, fifteen and eighteen stories high. For visitors to the area the district is a must. Here is to be found some of the most thrilling, non-stop gambling action—with a variety that ranges from slot machines to craps, keno, blackjack, roulette and even betting on horse races and ball games—and star-studded live entertainment. At virtually any hour of the day or night, one can see casino-goers bobbing along the sidewalks here, stalking in and out of clubs, courtesy buses darting back and forth between the clubs and the motels, tour buses giving out-of-area residents a preview of the district, and yellow cabs preying for fares at the casino-entrances. You can walk beneath marquees featuring some of the biggest and most glamorous names in the entertainment world, and dine in some excellent gourmet restaurants, as well as modest, cafe-style eateries. Most of the shows, too, are moderately priced, and well worth it.

There are five hotel-casinos in the district—Harrah's Tahoe, Harvey's Resort Hotel, Caesar's Tahoe, the High Sierra and Bill's—with two others, Lakeside Inn and Casino and John's Tahoe Nugget, lying just outside the district at the foot of the Kingsbury Grade. Oldest on the block is Harvey's, propped right up at the stateline with barely inches to spare between its west wall and the State of California (where gambling, as practiced in Reno and Las Vegas, is illegal). Harvey's has actually grown out of an early day gambling establishment of sorts, the Wagon Wheel Saloon, which first appeared on the scene, upon this very site, in 1946, opening for business with a six-stool counter, three slot machines, two pool tables, and a 24-hour gas pump to lure the occasional motorist. In 1960, gaming pioneer Harvey Gross, for whom the casino is named, built the present-day 11-story, 200-room resort hotel which, most notably, became Lake Tahoe's first highrise. More recently, however, the addition of a new 22-story, 547-room wing to the original hotel has given Harvey's yet another distinction—it is now the tallest building at the lake. Worth visiting at Harvey's is the Top of the Wheel restaurant and lounge which offers unparalleled, panoramic views of the lake and the Sierras. Also of interest at the hotel is a glass elevator which, again, offers some great views of the lake as it climbs

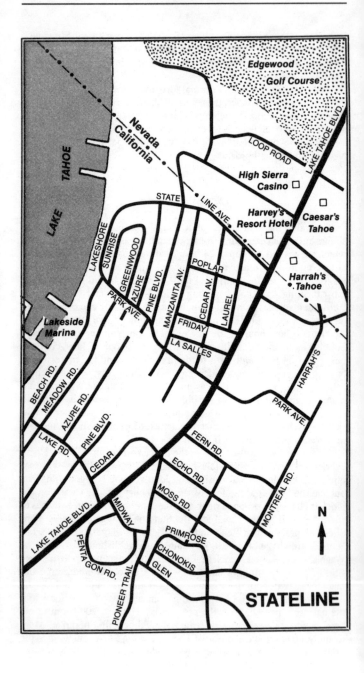

from the casino floor to the Top of the Wheel.

Directly across the street from Harvey's is the Harrah's Tahoe Hotel-Casino, with its out-size parking lot spilling over into the California side, offering a unique opportunity for driving into the club through one state and leaving via another. Harrah's is 18 stories high, built in 1973 by Bill Harrah, who in the late 1950's, after building the Harrah's Reno Hotel, was glamorized as "the biggest gambler in the world," until Howard Hughes went on his historic buying spree in Las Vegas in the mid-1960's and wrested the title. The hotel boasts 540 well-appointed guest rooms and over 70,000 square feet of casino space. Of particular interest at Harrah's is The Summit lounge and restaurant, from where spectacular, all-round views of Lake Tahoe can be enjoyed.

Adjoining the Harrah's hotel on the east is the Harrah's Sportsbook, a tiny extension of the main building, which caters to betting on horse races and ball games. And to the east of there is Bill's, the smallest club on the block. Bill's is actually part of the Harrah's hotel chain, named, again, for Bill Harrah, founder of Harrah's Hotel-Casino.

Farther east from Harrah's and Bill's is to be found the glamorous Caesar's Tahoe, part of the Caesar's Palace, Las Vegas chain. Caesar's is a 15-story hotel with a worthwhile shopping arcade and one or two delightful restaurants, including Le Posh which is billed as "one of the most elegant restaurants in Northern Nevada." Across the street from Caesar's stands the 14-story High Sierra Hotel-Casino, formerly known as the Sahara. The High Sierra was originally built in 1965.

East of the casino district, a little way, are the two "outlying" clubs, Lakeside Inn and Casino and John's Tahoe Nugget, both relatively small but with good gambling possiblities and live entertainment.

The California Side

The California side of the Stateline, especially the section between Stateline Avenue and Park Avenue, is among the most densely populated parts of South Lake Tahoe, best explored on foot. The Lake Tahoe Boulevard runs through the midst of here, as elsewhere in the city, and alongside of it are to be seen several specialty shops, most of them peddling Tahoe souvenirs in every shape, size and color. Three or four well-equipped sporting goods stores can found along here too, and a handful of restaurants, with one or two of them located on the highway, are worth visiting as well. During the summer one can even find tiny "information" booths dotting the sidewalks along here, freely dispensing timeshare condominium literature. North of Lake Tahoe Boulevard, down to Lakeside Avenue, is "motel country," where scores of motels, all vying for the tourist trade beneath bright-eyed "vacancy" signs, stand shoulder to shoulder on the half-dozen or so little streets criss-crossing through there. South of the boulevard on Park Avenue is the Crescent V Shopping Center, and at the lake end of Park Avenue is the Lakeside Marina, a favorite with summer vacationers, which has some boating possibilities. Interestingly, during the 1860's and 1870's, Lakeside was the site of Lapham's Hotel and Landing, and the stateline was thought to run through the center of it; but four decades and four surveys later, the stateline was established some 2000 feet to the northeast.

Heavenly Valley

Heavenly Valley is a place of superlatives: it is America's largest alpine ski resort; it has the highest skiable point at the lake, atop Monument Peak, elevation 10,100 feet; and it boasts one of the steepest ski trails in America, the Motts Canyon Trail, located in Heavenly North on the Nevada side. The ski resort is actually sprawled over nine different mountains comprising more than 20 square miles. It is unique in that a third of it lies in California and two-thirds in Nevada, with a ski trail leading over the top of it, enabling one to ski from one state to the other. There are three base lodges here—the California Base Lodge, and Stagecoach and Boulder—and a handful of day lodges perched at higher elevations. Heavenly, in addition, boasts some 26 chair lifts and over 100 ski runs, the oldest of which, Gunbarrel, originally opened to skiers in December of 1955. Of particular interest at Heavenly, however, is the aerial tram, which takes one from the California Base Lodge to the delightful Top of the Tram restaurant, some 2000 feet above lake level, with splendid, panoramic views of the lake and the surrounding mountains to be enjoyed enroute. Interestingly, the 50-passenger tram cars travel along a cable length of 1400 feet to achieve a vertical rise of 1700 feet. The tram ride takes 3 minutes and 38 seconds to the top.

Also to be found on the California side, just below the ski resort, are some excellent lodging facilities, including the Heavenly Valley Townhouses, and the delightful Christiania Inn, which, by the way, also has a restaurant. In the vicinity, too, are a half-dozen or so ski shops, most of them on Ski Run Boulevard, on the way to the Heavenly ski resort; and located at the top of the boulevard is Hansen's Resort, which has a sled hill and saucer and sled rentals. Hansen's also has accommodations.

THE SOUTHEAST CORNER

The southeast corner of the lake, quite in contrast to the dazzling Stateline and the equally vibrant city area, is made up of a dozen or so tiny, independent, and more or less rural communities, among them Edgewood, Round Hill, Zephyr Cove, Cave Rock, Logan Shoals, Glenbrook and Kingsbury. An attempt to explore these, however, involves two separate excursions: one north along the shoreline; the other east over the Kingsbury Grade.

Kingsbury Grade

The Kingsbury Grade is just to the southeast of the Stateline casinos, off Highway 50. It is noted for its spectacular drive which takes the motorist on a steep ascent to the Daggett Summit (elevation 7375 feet), then in a dramatic plunge down the Haines Canyon and into the Carson Valley, a descent of some 3000 feet, achieved in just over 6 miles. Along the way a great deal of scenery can be enjoyed, with a Lookout Point being reached about halfway down the mountain, from where views of the Carson Valley and its green rectangles of farmland dotted with tiny brown farm-houses, are breathtaking. The Kingsbury Grade also has some historic merit. The travel route over the grade was first built in 1860 as part of the original Overland Pony Express Route, and named for its builder, David Demmen Kingsbury. In fact, this is the historic Kingsbury-Daggett Pass Cut-off over which the Bonanza traffic of the 1860's passed.

In any event, on the west face of Kingsbury Grade, directly above the Highway 50 turnoff, is the small, self-contained Kingsbury Village, and adjacent to it, Tahoe Village, where you can see, at its eastern end, some fascinating mountain construction, with homes and condominium complexes virtually clinging to the edge of the mountain, overlooking Carson Valley thousands of feet below. Several splendid resort developments such as the Tahoe Sierra Resort and the Tahoe Seasons Resort, are to be found here too. Heavenly Valley North adjoins just to the back of Tahoe Village, reached via Benjamin Drive.

On the eastern side, just to the south at the bottom of the grade, of course, lie the twin townships of Minden and Gardnerville, the latter especially notable for its Basque influence. Close at hand, too, is the historic Walley's Hot Springs Resort, dating from 1862, and a little to the north at the foot of the grade lies Genoa, Nevada's oldest settlement, where a group of Mormons established a trading post in 1849. At Genoa one can visit gaming pioneer Harvey Gross' ranch, famous for its herds of bison.

Edgewood to Zephyr Cove

Northeast of the Stateline lies Edgewood, not an essentially populous community, but with a golf course of considerable interest. The Edgewood Golf Course, rated by *Golf Digest* as one of the top ten public courses in the country, is an 18-hole, 7563-yard championship course with three-quarters of a mile of beach frontage, accessible from Loop Road, south of which stands the High Sierra Hotel-Casino.

Directly across from the Edgewood Golf Course, situated in an open meadow on the east side of the highway, is the historic Friday's Station, a charming, Bonanza era hostelry, characteristic in its hand-hewn posts and rails, originally built in 1860 by one "Friday" Burke, for whom it is named. In the 1860's this was also a Pony Express stop, with "Pony Bob" Haslem, one of the most celebrated Pony Express riders, headquartered here. The hostelry is now a private home, beautifully restored by its owners. It can be viewed from the highway, or Loop Road.

It is approximately one and one-half miles from Edgewood to Round Hill (also known as Round Mound), where a well-rounded knoll, some 500 feet above lake level, can be seen on the west side of the highway. Round Hill, too, is a more or less self-contained community, with a shopping mall and one or two worthwhile restaurants. Below the Round Mound, however, lies Nevada Beach, a lovely stretch of yellow sand with some picnicking possibilities, and to the east of there is Elk Point, a small tract of land jutting out into the lake.

Above Elk Point, of course, is secluded Marla Bay, and to its north, Zephyr Point and the sheltered, crescent-shaped Zephyr Cove. This last, Zephyr Cove, although named for the strong afternoon winds that sometimes sweep across it from the Emerald Bay gorge and the Rubicon Range in the west, is really a lovely little summer resort, with a delightful sandy beach and marina. It is, besides, also the home port of the *M.S. Dixie*, Lake Tahoe's oldest cruise boat in service, which made its debut on the lake in 1947. The *Dixie*, much like the *Tahoe Queen*, is a glass-bottomed, Mississippi river-boat, quite picturesque with its giant red paddlewheel. The *Dixie* offers a variety of cruises, to Emerald Bay and around the lake. Also berthed at Zephyr Cove is the large trimaran, *Woodwind*, quite possibly the largest sailing vessel at the lake; it, too, offers lake cruises in the summer, sailing quite randomly into the sunset. Zephyr Cove also has a campground, a lodge, riding stables, and a handful of shops and a general store nestled along the highway.

Cave Rock

Leaving Zephyr Cove the highway travels almost directly north for some 4 miles, at the end of which one encounters a large promontory — the legendary Cave Rock, a volcanic neck formed nearly 5 million years ago. The rock has two tunnels passing through it, one naturally formed and the other man-made, with the highway passing through both. The man-made tunnel was built in the early 1900's, and the other was created in times immemorable by the Great Spirit thrusting his lance into the rock. And here, again, is a romantic Indian legend tracing the formation of the original cave. According to the legend, there once lived a tribe of Washoe Indians by the rock, fishing and hunting for the most part. The tribe lived in great harmony and peace. Then one day, as the story goes, the lake waters began to rise and the tribe scrambled for high ground. But the lake waters continued to rise and the tribespeople climbed higher, above the rock. And the waters rose higher still. So then the tribespeople looked to the Great Spirit for help, and the Great Spirit responded by thrusting his lance into the rock to form a cave for the waters to drain into. And thus the waters receded and the tribe was saved. But then another problem arose: the water rushing into the cave created a suction into which many of the tribe's fishermen drifted, and were lost. So once again the tribe looked to the Great Spirit for guidance, and the Great Spirit asked the tribesmen to choose the strongest among them for a task of great magnitude. And the tribe chose a brave named "Bo-ha-ra-te". The Great Spirit then placed a

Heavenly Valley's aerial tram offers panoramic views of the lake

Emerald Bay, Lake Tahoe

large tree-stump by the cave and instructed "Bo-ha-ra-te" to move it across the mouth of the cave every time a fishing boat neared. Thus another disaster was averted, and the tribe lived peacefully once again.

Cave Rock is also believed to have been the site of several pitched battles between the Washoe and the Paiute, and a legend stemming from this belief holds that a peace-loving people (the Washoe) were once made captive by a cruel, warring tribe (the Paiute), and that the "god of the world" came to the rescue of the peace-loving people, creating a cave in the rock in which to imprison the wicked people. The cave then came to be known as the "Prison of the Genii."

A rest area located near the rock, roughly 200 feet below the highway, has some splendid views of the lake, as well as excellent inshore fishing along the banks. Of interest, too, is the west face of Cave Rock, on which it is possible to discern the profile of a lady, known as the "Lady of the Lake," with distinctive eye lashes, a delicately upturned nose and a rose-bud mouth. This is best seen from the water when traveling to the rock by boat from the north. A larger profile, that of a gorilla, can also be discerned just above the "Lady of the Lake."

There is a small residential community at Cave Rock, and north of there lies Logan Shoals, with a public launching ramp for boating enthusiasts.

North to Glenbrook

From Cave Rock it is 4 miles to historic Glenbrook, the site of Lake Tahoe's first shoreline sawmill, and the largest lumbering settlement in the 1870's and 1880's. In its heyday, Glenbrook boasted one of the lake's most splendid hostelries, the Glenbrook House, while some of the area's finest steamers, including the legendary *Tahoe*, were berthed here too. The settlement, then, was also visited by such personages as Presidents Ulysses S. Grant and Rutherford B. Hayes, and humorist Mark Twain. Glenbrook is now a sleepy, privately owned retreat, with a 9-hole golf course and some tennis courts.

At Glenbrook, Highway 50 turns east and passes over Spooner Summit, where the Summit Mill, one of the area's earliest lumbermills, was built just prior to 1860. Also, near the Spooner Junction (intersection of Highways 50 and 28) is to be seen the site of the Spooner Station, a Bonanza era hostelry, built in 1863. An enchanting full-day hiking trail now meanders through the state park here. There is also a lake here, the Spooner Lake.

THE EMERALD BAY ROUTE

The Emerald Bay Route comprises essentially the Emerald Bay Road section of Highway 89, from just below the South Tahoe "Y" to the majestic Emerald Bay some 8 miles northwest, plus one or two worthwhile diversions, including Fallen Leaf Lake due south. The route is exceptionally scenic, quite splendid from the moment it leaves the city area. Endless groves of lush evergreens line the highway, punctuated in the fall with bursts of golden aspen; tiny snowmelt creeks can be seen toppling in thin, silver strands from the high country, then criss-crossing through the vast wooded meadows below; superb picture-postcard views of the lake can be enjoyed from several points along the highway, especially stunning where the highway hugs the shoreline; and to the west of the road rise a series of noble mountain peaks, including Mount Tallac which is the highest peak on Lake Tahoe's shoreline, and the twin Maggies Peaks. Then, too, there are dozens of lovely, shaded picnic areas and campgrounds to be encountered along the way, as well as two places of considerable historical interest, the Tallac Historic Site and the fabled Vikingsholm. There are, in addition, three delightful granite sand beaches to be found along the shoreline here, and a 2½-mile bike path that follows alongside of the highway, crossing over tiny, rustic bridges. Farther west from the route lies the infinitely remote, 63,469-acre Desolation Wilderness, with its many enchanting walks, circling scores of miniature fishing lakes. Indeed, this is one of the most scenic, unspoilt parts of Lake Tahoe, with much to offer the visitor.

Camp Richardson

Leaving the city area northwest on Emerald Bay Road, one first arrives at Camp Richardson, a lovely picture-book village with one lodge, one store and a handful of other structures dating from the early 1900's, largely unchanged in nearly 60 years. This was once known as "Camp Chipmunk," for the abundance of chipmunks to be found here in the summertime, and later on, in the 1930's and 1940's, it became "the favorite rural residence of city folk" due to its idyllic country setting. Originally, however, in the 1880's, Camp Richardson was a logging camp and also the site of Lake Tahoe's first steam-powered narrow-gauge railroad, the tracks from which can now be viewed at the neighboring Tallac Historic Site. Of interest, too, are the dozen or so barn-red cabins situated on the lake side of the highway, built mostly in the 1930's by one A.L. Richardson, an early day stageline operator who, in the early 1900's owned much of the acreage here, and for whom the camp is now named. At the fronts of these cabins are to be seen name plaques, each bearing a distinctive name of a bus or motor or other equipment that had served Richardson well during his staging years, such as Nash, Cord, Faegol, Devaux, Fleetwood, Packard, Plymouth, Pierce Arrow, Hall-Scott, and the like; most of these cabins have now been renovated and refurbished, and are available for vacation rental. Camp Richardson also has a notable campground, with 230 well-wooded campsites, and a full-service marina and resort, recently remodeled to accommodate a rambling, on-the-lake restaurant, the Beacon. Well known, too, are the Camp Richardson Stables, from where horseback trail rides can be taken through the adjoining back country. A delightful sandy beach, Pope Beach, lies just to the east of the camp.

Tallac Historic Site

Adjoining Camp Richardson on the west is the Tallac Historic Site, comprising, roughly, a 2000-acre estate, sweeping across from the edge of Camp Richardson to Mount Tallac farther west, and south from the Tahoe shoreline to the northern reaches of Fallen Leaf Lake. There are several points of interest here, notable among which is the Kiva Beach Recreation Area, a National Forest preserve situated about three-quarters of a mile west of Camp Richardson, and reached via a small side road, north off the highway. Kiva is a lovely, yellow sand beach, backing onto a magnificent grove of 200-year-old pines, believed to be among the oldest such stands of virgin timber in the Tahoe basin. Here amid the pines is also to be found the site of the legendary Tallac, a palatial three and one-half story hotel, known, in its heyday, as the "Saratoga of the Pacific." It was here that the well-heeled crowds of the 1890's and early 1900's gathered, creating an aura of fantastic high living in the Sierra Nevada. The Tallac was built in 1898 by Elias J. "Lucky" Baldwin, one of the most colorful personalities of his time, whose name is practically synonymous with the Tallac Estates. Much has been said and written about Baldwin over the years, and a tale is often told about how he came to be known as "Lucky." As the story goes, Baldwin, in his younger days, was just a stagecoach captain, with little to his name, save for some worthless mining stock he had earlier acquired in the Comstock for pennies. Then one day, he left on an out-of-area hunting trip, and asked a friend to sell off his stock for whatever it would fetch, for by then it had plummetted to new lows. But as it turned out, the stock certificates were locked up in a safe, the key to which Baldwin had taken with him—an honest error of omission. So the stock remained unsold. And as luck would have it, at about that time the mining company struck a fabulously rich vein of silver, and Baldwin's worthless stock turned into a fortune, almost overnight. Thus returned Elias Jackson Baldwin from his hunting trip a wealthy man, and a lucky one at that; and from that time on he came to be known as "Lucky."

Just to the east of the Tallac site are the historic estates of some notables from South Tahoe's past, including the Popes, the Tevises, the McGonagles, and even the Baldwins. Several graveled walks meander through here, with rock gardens and little streams crossed over by tiny, wooden bridges to be seen here and there, interspersed with a serene pergola or two. Three elaborate homes, dating from the early 1900's and featuring wrap-around covered porches and rocked-in fountains, can be toured here as well. A couple of turn-of-the-century boathouses dot the estates' sandy shoreline, with one of them housing the original rail tracks from the historic Camp Richardson Railroad. Situated on the water's edge, too, is a charming "Honeymoon Cottage," built from hand-hewn logs and molded tree limbs, with panoramic glass windows looking out over the lake. Also to be found on the grounds is an ancient but well-preserved log structure that houses the Tallac Museum. This is open to the public during summer, and it has on display a wealth of old photographs and other memorabilia from the Tallac past. During summer also, several cultural events and art exhibits are featured at the

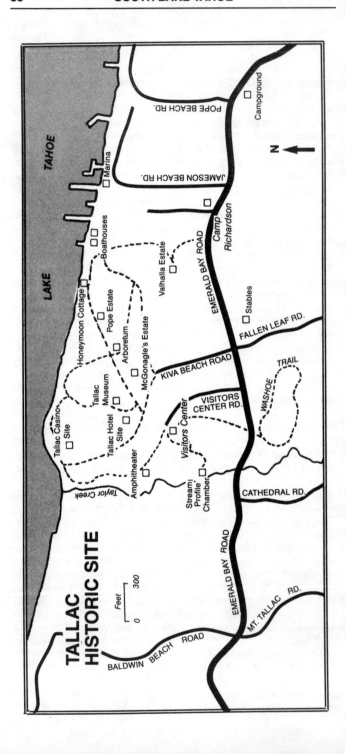

estates.

West of the Kiva Beach Recreation Area lies the U.S. Forest Service Visitor Center, reached via another side road, just 300 feet from the Kiva Beach turnoff. The Visitor Center is especially interesting to nature buffs and children, and has some educational merit. Here one can visit a "stream profile chamber" —a glass-enclosed area at stream level—located at Taylor Creek, and where native Kokanee Salmon can be viewed in their natural habitat. The Kokanee, of course, spawn farther upstream, swimming up from the lake in the fall, thus October is one of the best months to view them. Also of interest here is a short, 15-minute walk that circles to the back of the Visitor Center and leads to the Taylor Creek inlet point, passing by a miniature amphitheater enroute, where picture slide shows are often featured in the summer; until only a few decades ago, Washoe Indians used to camp by the influx of the creek into the lake. Another worthwhile walk, the "Washoe Trail," which starts out from the Visitor Center parking area and leads across to the south side of the highway, depicts the life-styles and survival methods of the Washoe Indians, especially interesting to those inclined toward Native American culture.

Southwest from the Visitor Center rises the mighty Mount Tallac, the highest peak on the lake's shoreline, with an elevation of 9785 feet. Tallac means "Great Mountain," and it is for this mountain that the estates are named. The mountain is also noted for its "snow-cross" (a cross-shaped indent filled with snow), which can be seen on its northeastern face. A hiking trail leads to the base of the mountain, and for the stout of heart there is even a trail journeying to the summit. North of Mount Tallac, of course, some three miles away, is Baldwin Beach, another fine, granite sand beach.

Fallen Leaf Lake

5 miles south of Emerald Bay Road lies Fallen Leaf Lake, a pleasant little summer retreat, arrived at by taking Fallen Leaf Road—the turnoff for which is to be found almost directly across from the Kiva Beach turnoff—to the very end. Fallen Leaf Lake is actually the second largest alpine lake in the region, second only to Lake Tahoe. It is approximately three miles long and a mile wide, with a depth of around 420 feet. The lake is believed to have been formed thousands of years ago by a feeder glacier that later joined the main body of ice in the Lake Tahoe trough, and is named for a Delaware chief, "Falling Leaf," who was the guide for Colonel John C. "Cockeye" Johnson, the trailblazing pioneer of the Sierra, of Johnson Pass Cut-off fame. An enchanting Indian legend, however, has quite another, rather fascinating version as to the formation and the naming of the lake. According to it, an Indian brave fleeing from the Evil One was given a branch of a tree by the Good Spirit, each leaf of which, when dropped on the ground, would create a body of water, thus imposing a barrier before the Indian brave's pursuer, the Evil One. As the Indian fled, crossing over what is now the eastern Sierra range, the Evil One closed in on him. The Indian panicked, and in his attempt to break off a leaf, he broke off the entire

branch, save for one leaf, and dropped it on the ground; and where the branch fell, the great Lake Tahoe was created. The Indian continued west. But soon, as he approached Mount Tallac, he looked back to see that the Evil One had circled the lake's south shore and was once again closing in on him. So now the Indian dropped that last leaf he still clutched in his hand, and in its place sprang Fallen Leaf Lake. The Indian then safely crossed over into the Valley of the Sacramento, and the lake came to be known as Fallen Leaf, for that magical fallen leaf that had created it.

Fallen Leaf Lake is a more or less self-contained resort, noted primarily for its lodge, nestled along its southeast corner. The Fallen Leaf Lodge, a brown-shingled two-story building dating from 1913, was built by William Whitman Price, naturalist and Stanford University professor, who ran a boys summer camp in these parts in as early as 1905. A boathouse and marina are located just across from the lodge, and set farther back are several summer cabins, many of them dating from 1911. Both the lodge and cabins are now privately owned, however.

Fallen Leaf is also an excellent fishing lake, and an ideal base from which to explore the idyllic Desolation Wilderness that adjoins to the west. Dozens of secluded trails through the wilderness are accessible from here, including ones to Lily, Heather and the Azure lakes. Southeast of the lake is to be found the Angora Lookout (elevation approximately 7000 feet), which offers breathtaking views of Lake Valley below. A short distance to the west of Fallen Leaf one can visit the Floating Island Lake, where a real floating island can be seen; the island is said to have provided early day fishermen with a quiet approach when fishing in the tiny lake. Just beyond the floating island, a trail threads past clumps of pine and fir to lead to the base of Mount Tallac in the northwest.

Cascade Lake and Emerald Bay

Returning to our main route of travel, Highway 89, just to the northwest of the Tallac Historic Site the road begins to climb sharply, weaving around a handful of hairpin bends and skirting the entrances to the Eagle Point and Emerald Bay campgrounds to the south, then passes over a vertical ridge that offers a unique view of two infinitely beautiful bodies of water: Cascade Lake and Emerald Bay.

Cascade Lake, which lies to the south of the ridge and is often to be seen frozen over in winter, is the smaller of the two, about a mile long and a half mile wide. The lake is picturesque in a rugged sort of way, and in the 1930's and 1940's it also provided the setting for some early day wilderness movies, such as *Lightnin'*, starring Will Rodgers, *Rose Marie*, starring Jeannette McDonald and Nelson Eddy, and Dreiser's *A Place in the Sun*. Earlier, in the 1890's and early 1900's, personages such as Mark Twain, John Muir, and Sybil Sanderson, the noted chanteusse, came to stroll the Cascade shores, attracted by its singular beauty; and in 1926, John Steinbeck, then a fledgling student at Stanford, spent the entire summer here. The lake, however, is named for the majestic waterfalls in its southwest corner, seen cascading in 100-foot drops down naked granite ledges, to plunge into the lake in a wash of white; these are especially spectacular in the spring, when the feeder stream is full and roiling. The falls are actually known as the White Cloud Falls, and during the Bonanza Period (1860's) they were the focus of many an artist. Some of the finished canvases featuring these are said to have fetched as much as $2000 in those days.

In centuries past, Cascade Lake was a favorite campsite of the Washoe Indians. It was then known as "Wa-su-sha-te," meaning "Good Fishing Lake," for its reputation for fishing, at the time, rivalled that of neighboring Fallen Leaf Lake and the smaller Desolation Wilderness lakes. Cascade Lake is also believed to have been the scene of a fierce and bloody battle between the Washoe and Paiute Indian tribes, in which even the women and children are said to have partaken. Several arrowheads and broken bits of spears have been found here since, mainly in the 1800's. In 1880, even a mummified body of an Indian squaw, we are told, was found buried by the edge of the lake, remarkably well preserved by the extreme cold temperatures of the water. At the time of its discovery, the bloated body, reportedly, weighed nearly 300 pounds.

Cascade Lake is now privately owned, the acreage having been first acquired in the mid-1880's by Dr. Charles Brooks Bringham, a noted San Francisco surgeon. It has since passed on to his heirs and family, whose summer homes dot the lake's northeastern shoreline.

Directly north of Cascade Lake lies the famous Emerald Bay, acknowledged as "the most beautiful inland harbor in the world." Emerald Bay, quite like the Fallen Leaf and Cascade lakes, was carved out during the ice age by a feeder glacier that eventually joined the main body of ice in Lake Tahoe. The bay is named for its entrancing blue-green waters, and it is today one of the most photographed spots in the Tahoe basin. It is also a favorite destination for the area's cruise boats, which feature year-round Emerald Bay cruises. In the center of the bay is a tiny island, a pinnacled granite outcropping rising some 150 feet from the water. This is Lake Tahoe's only island, variously known as Coquette, Hermit's, Fannette and Emerald Isle. On the island sits a one-room stone "tea house," with a lovely miniature fireplace to be viewed within, built in about 1930; and beside the "tea house" is the site of a long decayed wooden, Gothic tomb, originally built in the 1930's by one Captain Richard Barter, a hard-drinking, hard-swearing English salt, also known as "the Hermit of Emerald Bay." Barter was the caretaker for the Emerald Bay estates for several years, and was notorious for his frequent boating accidents which inevitably followed his drinking. On one occasion, according to local lore, he nearly froze to death after his boat capsized just outside the bay. Upon returning to his quarters at the head of the bay, however, he found his toes to be frost-bitten, and—believe it or not—he then proceeded to amputate them with a kitchen knife. In any event, locals will tell you that on cold, dark nights a wispy mist rises from the bay, almost directly above the island, and that that is the ghost of Captain Barter, looking for his tomb.

At the head of Emerald Bay is to be found the Eagle Falls Picnic Area, and to the back of there are viewed the magnificent Eagle Falls, tumbling in three successive falls down to the lake; the falls are fed by the tiny Eagle Lake, located in the high country Desolation Wilderness. The head of the bay also offers some of the most spectacular views of the bay and the lake beyond, especially striking at sunrise when the eastern skies directly across are a flaming amber. It is interesting also to note that the road at the head of the bay was the last section of the Rim of the Lake Road to be completed, opening to traffic in 1913. The present highway is actually cut into the face of the lower Maggies Peak, and is frequently closed in winter due to rock slides. During its construction, reportedly, several of the largest boulders had to be blasted four or five times each, before they would be moved, such was the task of building this section of the road.

Just to the north of the head of the bay is a car park, from where a mile-long trail descends into the cradle of the bay. It is a somewhat steep trail, but well worth the effort, for at the end of it lies one of Lake Tahoe's greatest treasures: Vikingsholm.

Vikingsholm

Vikingsholm is a masterful replica of a 1200-year-old Viking castle, billed as "the finest example of Scandinavian architecture in North America". Built in 1929 by Lora Josephine Knight, heiress to several fortunes, the castle displays the splendor of an ancient and majestic era. Two turreted towers flank the rock and mortar facade of the main house, and a north wing and south wing, constructed wholly from wood, extend to the back of the house to form an open courtyard, quite artfully landscaped with rocks and trees. The roofs of the two extension wings are covered with sod, especially picturesque in spring when native wildflowers sprout lavishly upon the sod. In the Viking days the sod served as a form of insulation, and was trimmed by allowing goats to graze upon it. On the east side of the courtyard buildings, sharpened rafters jut out from under the roof, supposedly there to ward off evil spirits. Also to be seen on some of the extension buildings are "dragon crosses," uniquely Norwegian. These date back a thousand years or more, to the time when Christianity was first being introduced in the Scandinavian lands; the dragon heads were, in fact, an accommodation of Norwegian superstitions, and were allowed to remain for that added protection against evil spirits.

During the summer months the State Parks Department conducts tours through the interior of Vikingsholm, with a guide narrating the history of the castle and tales and legends from the Viking era. Within Vikingsholm are to be seen several marvelous duplications of Scandinavian antiques, furniture and other fixtures, and authentic Norwegian weavings. On the ground floor, hanging from the ceiling of the living room are two intricately carved "dragon" beams; in the Viking era the area directly beneath the beams was the exclusive domain of the chieftain and his most honored guests, with women and children being excluded from it. Also in the living room is a lovely, hand-painted "Bridal Chest," given to newlyweds under Norwegian custom, and adorning the living room wall is an exquisite Oriental rug, reportedly

VIKINGSHOLM

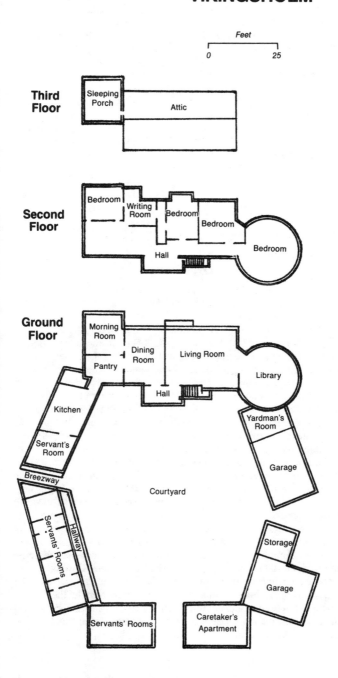

purchased for $40,000 in 1929. Farther in, in the hallway stands a life-size wood-carving of a Finnish peasant girl, "Selma," with a clock for its face (a typically Swedish art form). Also in the hallway is a closet door, quite interesting in its fine floral designs. On the upper floor are five individually decorated bedrooms, three of them featuring Norwegian stone fireplaces. Also on this floor is a small but interesting "writing room," situated just off the end bedroom, which forms that curious wooden projection seen at the front of the mansion, along the upper right corner; the use of such wooden projections was dominant in early day Norwegian churches.

At the front of Vikingsholm are a boathouse and an L-shaped pier, making the castle accessible by boat as well. Vikingsholm can also be reached by way of a 4-mile hiking trail, the Rubicon Trail, which starts out from the adjoining D.L. Bliss State Park to the north, offering some scenic views of the lake enroute.

DETOURS

Carson City

A worthwhile detour for visitors to South Lake Tahoe is Carson City, located some 27 miles to the northeast, at the intersection of Highways 395 and 50, more or less at the foot of the eastern Sierra. Carson City, most significantly, is the smallest state capital in the nation, with a population of around 15,000. It is also rich in historic buildings and old, Victorian mansions. Of particular interest here are the Governor's Mansion, situated on Mountain Street, and the Nevada State Museum, located on Carson Street and considered to be one of the finest museums in the West. The museum is housed in the old U.S. Mint building, dating from 1866, where silver was coined during the Comstock era, and it has on display a wealth of 19th-century artifacts and the controversial "Fremont Cannon." Other places of interest in Carson City include the State Capitol, the State Library and the Legislative Building, all of which are open to the public on weekdays. Also worth visiting are the Old Virginia & Truckee Railroad Shop, located at the corner of Stewart and Washington streets, and the Nevada State Supreme Court on Carson Street. Just south of Carson City lies the Railroad Museum, where antique trains and steam engines are being restored. Of interest, too, is the Ormsby House Hotel-Casino, a long-standing institution, once owned by U.S. Senator Paul Laxalt. The Carson City Visitors Center, by the way, is located in the Carson Shopping Mall, just south of town; self-guided maps with histories and detailed information on several restored homes are available at the center.

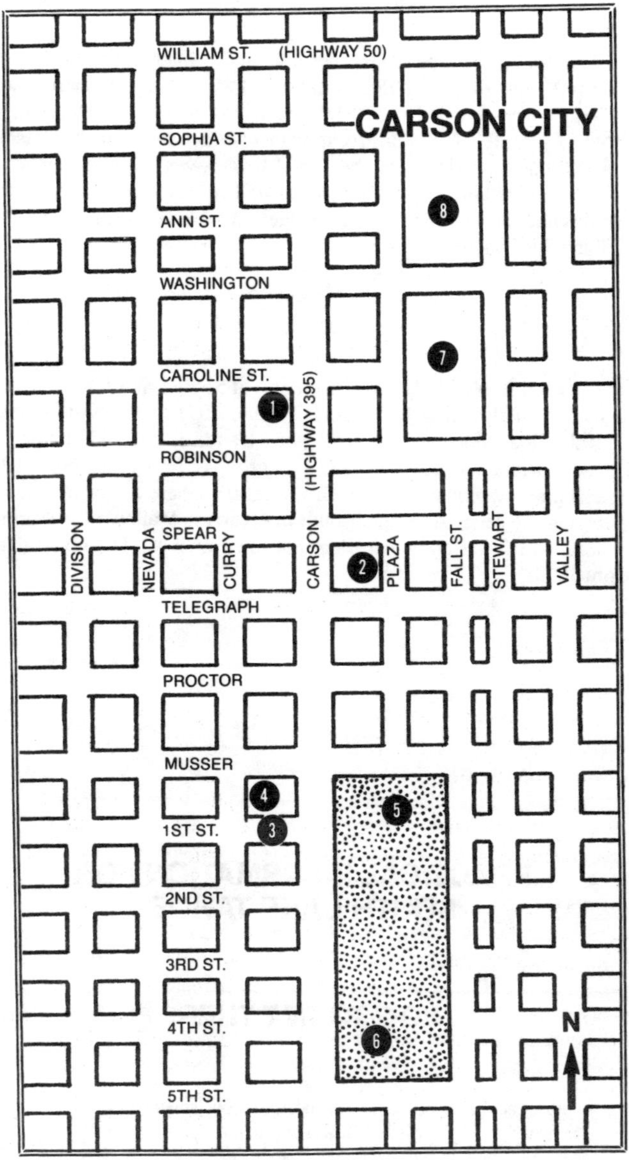

CARSON CITY

Points of Interest –
1) Nevada State Museum
2) Nevada State Library
3) Nevada State Supreme Court
4) Fire Department & Museum
5) State Capitol
6) State Legislative Building
7) Post Office and Federal Building
8) Old V & T Shop

Gardnerville and Minden

The twin townships of Gardnerville and Minden are nestled in the Carson Valley, some 18 miles from South Lake Tahoe, reached by way of Kingsbury Grade (Route 207) and Highway 395. Gardnerville is especially notable for its Basque influence, with some excellent Basque food restaurants to be found there. At Minden, visit Sharkey's Casino, where several antique slot machines and rodeo king Casey Tibbs' saddles and old photographs can be viewed, as well as some authentic Indian Chief portraits.

Genoa

Genoa lies roughly 12 miles northeast of South Lake Tahoe, arrived at by taking the Kingsbury Grade (Route 207) to the bottom, then Foothill Road northward a little way. Genoa is the oldest town in Nevada, originally settled in 1849 by a group of Mormons. Of interest here is gaming pioneer Harvey Gross' ranch, where a herd of real live bison can be seen. Also, just south of Genoa is Walley's Hot Springs Resort, which has some excellent hot mineral spas. The resort dates from 1862.

PRACTICAL INFORMATION FOR SOUTH LAKE TAHOE

HOW TO GET THERE

South Lake Tahoe lies 190 miles northeast of San Francisco, or 103 miles from Sacramento. The best and easiest way to reach it is by way of *Interstate 80* east from San Francisco to Sacramento, then *Highway 50* directly northeast to South Lake Tahoe. When journeying from the south, follow *Interstate 5* north to Sacramento, and *Highway 50* to South Lake Tahoe. An alternative route from the south is by way of *Highway 395* to Gardnerville, Nevada, and *Highways 207* and *50* westward to South Lake Tahoe.

South Lake Tahoe is serviced by *Greyhound* on a regular, daily basis, with scheduled departures and arrivals to and from most major cities. The Greyhound Bus Terminal is located on Park Avenue in the Stateline area, directly across from the Crescent V Shopping Center. For schedules and more information, call (916) 544-2241.

The city of South Lake Tahoe also has a commercial airport, situated on Highway 50, just south of the city (airport phone: 916-541-4080). The airport is serviced by *American Airlines* (800-433-7300/916-541-8360), which has regularly scheduled flights to South Lake Tahoe. Several other airlines fly to Reno International Airport (see *North Lake Tahoe* section), while at least two companies operate a shuttle-bus service between the Reno International Airport and South Lake Tahoe. *See Tahoe Tours* (702) 832-0713 and *LTR* (702) 323-4511.

TOURIST INFORMATION

South Lake Tahoe Chamber of Commerce, 3066 Lake Tahoe Blvd., South Lake Tahoe; (916) 541-5255. Tourist information brochures, including lodging and restaurant listings, and show information; also calendar of events. Accommodation reservations may be made through the *South Lake Tahoe Visitors Authority,* 1156 Ski Run Blvd. (cnr. Tamarack St.), South Lake Tahoe; (916) 544-5050/(800) 822-5922.

Tahoe-Douglas Chamber of Commerce, P.O. Box 401, Zephyr Cove, Nevada 89448; (702) 588-4591. Tourist literature, including schedule of local events, and listings for area accommodations and restaurants.

Carson City Tourism Board, 1937 N. Carson, Carson City; (702) 883-7442. Brochures, calendar of events, general tourist information.

Lake Tahoe Basin Management Unit, 870 Emerald Bay Road; (916) 573-2600. Visitor information, local interest brochures and books, hiking information and maps, wilderness permits.

Road Conditions. For information on winter driving conditions in the area, and chain controls and road closures, call (916) 577-3550.

ACCOMMODATIONS

Stateline Area

Ambassador Motor Lodge. *$32-$42.* 4130 Manzanita; (916) 544-6461. 57 rooms, TV, phones, beach.

Black Jack Motel. *$18-$30.* 985 Park Ave.; (916) 544-3902. 24 rooms, TV, phones.

Best Western Lake Tahoe Inn. *$49-$70.* 901 Park Ave., (916) 541-2010. 400 rooms, TV, phones. Close to casinos.

Best Western Station House Inn. *$78.* 901 Park Ave.; (916) 542-1101. 100 rooms, TV, phones, pool, beach, spa, restaurant.

Blue Jay Motor Lodge. *$42-$52.* 4133 Cedar; (916) 544-5231. 65 rooms,

TV, pool, beach, phones.

Caesar's Tahoe. *$95-$125*. Lake Tahoe Blvd., Stateline; (702) 588-3515/ (800) 648-3353. 15-story, five star hotel, part of the Caesar's Palace-Las Vegas chain, situated 100 yards or so east of Harrah's. 446 luxury hotel rooms, most with lake views. Casino and shopping arcade on premises; also 6 restaurants, tennis and raquetball courts, indoor pool, jacuzzis and weight room. Live entertainment.

Capri Motel. *$39-$53*. 932 Stateline; (916) 544-3665. 25 rooms, TV, pool, beach.

Carriage House Inn. *$36-$56*. 4135 Laurel; (916) 544-3045. 25 rooms, TV.

Casino Area Travelodge. *$52-$62*. 4003 Highway 50; (916) 541-5000. 66 rooms, TV, phones, pool.

Eagle's Nest Inn. *$125-$150*. Needle Peak Rd. (off Kingsbury Grade, at the end of Tramway Drive); (702) 588-6492. 20 luxury units, each with whirlpool and lake or valley views. Superb restaurant on premises, open for breakfast, lunch and dinner. Ideal location, adjacent to Heavenly Valley North.

Elm Inn. *$38-$48*. 4082 Highway 50; (916) 541-7900. 102 rooms, TV, phones, pool, spa, restaurant.

Fantasy Inn II. *$78-$128*. 924 Park Ave.; (916) 544-6767. Adult motel with 24 units, TV, phones, pool, in-room spa.

Flamingo Lodge. *$55-$80*. 3961 Lake Tahoe Blvd.; (916) 544-5288. 89 rooms, TV, phones, pool, spa, sauna, restaurant.

Harrah's Tahoe. *$100-$120*. Lake Tahoe Blvd., Stateline; (702) 588-6611/(800) 648-3773 from California. 540-room, 18-story luxury hotel, located directly across from Harvey's. 70,000-square-foot casino floor, 5 superb restaurants, indoor swimming pool, sauna and spas, nautilus center, shopping arcade. Big name entertainment.

Harvey's Resort Hotel. *$65-$125*. Lake Tahoe Blvd., Stateline; (702) 588-2411. 547-room, 22-story resort hotel. Casino, arcade, 7 restaurants, live entertainment. For show information and reservations, call (800) 648-3361.

The High Sierra. *$76-$86*. Lake Tahoe Blvd., Stateline; (702) 588-6211/(800) 648-3322. 14-story hotel-casino, located directly across from Caesar's. Five notable restaurants, live entertainment and dancing. Full casino.

Holiday Lodge. *$50-$65*. 4095 Laurel; (916) 544-4101. 148 rooms, TV, phones, pool, sauna.

La Baer Motor Lodge. *$48-$68*. 4133 Highway 50; (916) 544-2139. 33 rooms, TV, phones.

The Lodge. *$100-$115*. 3880 Pioneer Trail; (916) 541-6226. 66 condominium units, TV, phones, swimming pool, spa.

Lucky Lodge. *$38-$54*. 952 Stateline Ave.; (916) 544-3369. 21 rooms, TV, pool, beach.

Mark Twain. *$34-$40*. 947 Park Ave.; (916) 544-5733. 34 rooms, TV, phones, pool, spa; close to beach and casinos.

Olympic Motel. *$35-$45*. 3901 Pioneer Trail; (916) 541-2119. 32 units, TV, phones, swimming pool, hot tub.

Pacifica Lodge. *$45-$55*. 931 Park Ave.; (916) 544-4131. 67 rooms, TV, phones, pool, hot tub.

Red Carpet Inn. *$44-$54*. 4100 Highway 50; (916) 544-2261. 56 rooms, TV, phones, pool, spa, beach, restaurant.

Riviera Inn. *$35-$59*. 890 Stateline Ave.; (916) 544-3448. 40 rooms, TV, pool.

Royal Valhalla Motor Lodge. *$52-$69*. 4104 Lake Shore Blvd.; (916) 544-2233. 79 units, many with private balconies overlooking the lake; some kitchen units. TV, phones, heated pool and spa; private beach.

Shamrock Inn. *$28-$36*. 4127 Pine; (916) 541-7150. 142 rooms, TV, phones, pool, spa, beach.

Sierra House Inn. *$42-$48*. 968 Park Ave.; (916) 541-4800. 60 rooms, TV, phones, pool, spa, sauna, beach.

South Shore Inn. *$40-$50*. 3906 Pioneer Trail; (916) 544-1000. 22 rooms, TV, phones.

Stateline Travelodge. *$52-$62*. 4011 Highway 50; (916) 544-6000. TV, phones, pool.

Tahoe Colony Inn. *$38-$42*. 3794 Montreal; (916) 544-6481. 103 rooms, TV, phones, pool, spa, beach.

Tahoe Driftwood. *$34-$54*. 4115 Laurel Ave.; (916) 541-7400. 50 rooms, TV, phones, pool, beach, restaurant.

Tahoe Queen Motel. *$28-$52*. Poplar and Manzanita; (916) 544-2291. 29 rooms, TV, phones, pool, spa, beach.

Tahoe West Motor Lodge. *$38-$46*. 4082 Pine Ave.; (916) 544-6455. 59 rooms, TV, phones, pool, spa, sauna, beach.

Tally Ho Motel. *$28-$58*. 4060 Highway 50; (916) 544-3037. 37 rooms, TV, pool, spa, restaurant.

Tradewinds Motel. *$38-$48*. 944 Friday Street; (800) 544-1355/(916) 544-6459. 68 rooms, TV, phones, pool, hot tub.

Viking Motor Lodge. *$30-$45*. 4083 Cedar; (916) 541-5155. 58 rooms, TV, phones, pool, spa, beach.

City Area

Alta Vista Motel. *$23-$33*. 3622 Highway 50; (916) 544-2034. 17 rooms, TV.

Blue Lake Motel. *$36-$56*. 1055 Ski Run Boulevard; (916) 544-4853. 27 rooms, TV, pool, spa.

Brooke's Lodge. *$38-$58*. 3892 Highway 50; (916) 544-3642. 36 rooms, TV, phones, pool.

Bell Court Lodge. *$38-$58*. 3838 Highway 50; (916) 541-5400. 121 rooms, TV, phones, pool, restaurant.

Christiania Inn. *$85-$175*. Heavenly Valley; (916) 544-7337. 2 luxury units. 2-night minimum stay.

Fantasy Inn I. *$78-$128*. 3677 Lake Tahoe Blvd.; (916) 541-6666. 32 room adult motel, TV, phones, in-room spa.

Lakeland Village. *$65-$80*. 3535 Lake Tahoe Blvd.; (800) 822-5969/(916) 541-7711. 210 condominium units, TV, phones, pool, sauna, hot tub.

Inn by the Lake. *$95-$125*. 3300 Highway 50; (916) 542-0330. 100 rooms and suites, TV, phones, pool, sauna and hot tub.

Seven Eleven Motel. *$26-$42*. 3640 Lake Tahoe Blvd.; (916) 544-3640. 21 rooms, TV, phones, spa.

South Tahoe Travelodge. *$52-$62*. 3489 Highway 50; (800) 255-3050/(916) 544-5266. 59 rooms, TV, phones, pool.

Tahoe Beach and Ski Resort. *$105-$145*. 3601 Highway 50; (916) 541-6220. 120 units, with TV and phones. Pool, spa, hot tub, restaurant.

Tahoe Hacienda. *$42-$58*. 3820 Highway 50; (916) 541-3805. 32 rooms, some with fireplaces and jacuzzis; TV, phones, pool, spa.

Tahoe Marina Inn and Condominiums. *$79-$120*. Bijou Shopping Center, Highway 50; (800) 822-5922/(916) 541-2180. 76 units, with TV and phones, some fireplaces and lakeside balconies. Heated pool, sauna, private beach.

Tahoe Sands Inn. *$58-$70*. 3600 Lake Tahoe Blvd.; (916) 544-3476. 109 rooms, TV, phones, pool, spa, sauna, and restaurant.

Tahoe Seasons Resort. *$128 +*. Keller and Saddle Roads; (916) 541-6010. 160 units, including some 1-bedroom suites with in-room spas and kitchens. TV, phones, pool, hot tub, restaurant.

Emerald Bay Road Area

Emerald Motel. *$25-$35*. 515 Emerald Bay Road; (916) 544-5515. 9 rooms, TV, pool.

High Country Lodge. *$35-$40*. 1227 Highway 50; (916) 544-0508. 15 rooms, TV.

Lazy S Lodge. *$36-$71*. 609 Emerald Bay Road; (916) 541-0230. 21 rooms, TV, pool, hot tub. Also some cottages with fireplaces and kitchenettes.

Matterhorn Motel. *$38-$58*. 2187 Highway 50; (916) 541-0367. 18 rooms, TV, phones, pool and hot tub.

Richardson's Resort. *$49-$69*. Emerald Bay Rd., Camp Richardson; (916) 541-1801. Historic resort with 29 rooms, each with private bath, in main lodge, and a 7-unit motel. Also 40 cabins, some lakefront, all with private bath and kitchen, available by the week ($450-$875). Excellent restaurant, marina, beach, campground, riding stables and general store.

Silver Shadows Lodge. *$35-$125*. 1251 Highway 50; (916) 541-3575. 18 rooms, TV, pool, hot tub.

Star Lake Motel. *$49-$59*. 2446 Highway 50; (916) 544-6676. 17 rooms, some with kitchenettes; TV, pool.

Sundowner Motel. *$35-$45*. 121 Highway 50; (916) 541-2282. 16 rooms, TV, phones, restaurant next door.

Washoe Motel. *$30-$40*. 751 Emerald Bay Road; (916) 541-1141. 16 rooms, TV, pool, restaurant.

HOW TO GET AROUND

By Bus. The city of South Lake Tahoe is serviced by *STAGE* (South Tahoe Area Ground Express). A regular, 24-hour schedule is maintained between the Stateline and the South Tahoe Y, and scheduled stops are made at marked bus-stops along Lake Tahoe Boulevard. Buses may be flagged on any street serviced by *STAGE* except Lake Tahoe Boulevard. For a timetable and route information, call (916) 544-2266.

By Taxi. South Lake Tahoe has the following taxi companies: *South Tahoe Yellow Cabs* (916) 544-5555, *Checker Cab Co.* (916) 541-5151, *Tahoe Ready Cab* (916) 542-2424, *Sunshine Taxi Co.* (702) 588-5555 and *Dial-a-Ride* (916) 577-7000. *Dial-a-Ride* also offers charters and tours, in cars, buses and limousines.

By Car. Car rentals are available at *Avis Rent-A-Car*, (916) 541-7800; *Allstar Rent A Car*, (916) 544-0773; *Tahoe Rent-A-Car*, (916) 544-4500; *Budget*, (916) 541-5777/(702) 588-5145; *Hertz*, (702) 588-4911; and *Dollar Rent A Car*, (702) 588-4849. Most car rental agencies also rent four-wheel-drive vehicles, with snow tires, chains and ski-racks.

Shuttle Services. All the major casinos in the area have courtesy buses plying between the clubs and motels; for timetables, call the respective casino or inquire at your motel. Additionally, the *Tahoe Queen* (916) 541-3364 offers across-the-lake transportation to the north shore much of the year; and *See Tahoe Tours* (702-832-0713) as well as *LTR* (702-323-4511) operate shuttle-bus services between South Lake Tahoe and the Reno International Airport.

South Lake Tahoe enjoys a lovely alpine setting at the southern edge of Lake Tahoe

Vikingsholm, a replica of a 1200-year-old Scandinavian stone castle, sits at the head of Emerald Bay

Wooden boats at the Concours d'Elegance at Tahoe City

South Lake Tahoe's casino district at night

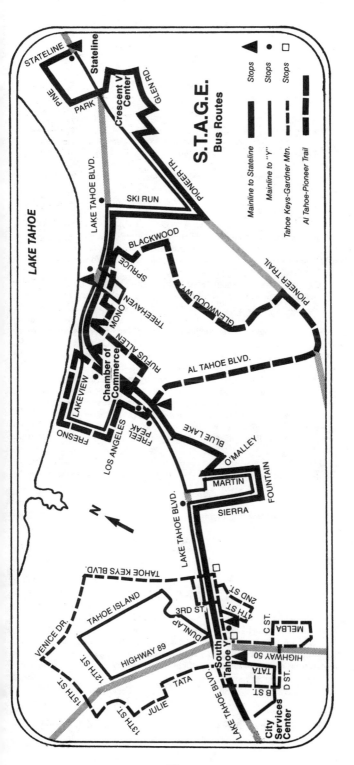

S.T.A.G.E.
Bus Routes

Stops ▶
Stops •
Stops □

— Mainline to Stateline
— Mainline to "Y"
- - - Tahoe Keys-Gardner Mtn.
▬▬▬ Al Tahoe-Pioneer Trail

LAKE TAHOE

STATELINE
PINE
PARK
Stateline
Crescent V Center
GLEN RD.
PIONEER TR.
SKI RUN
LAKE TAHOE BLVD.
BLACKWOOD
SPRUCE
TREEHAVEN
MONO
RUFUS ALLEN
GLENWOOD WY.
PIONEER TRAIL
AL TAHOE BLVD.
Chamber of Commerce
LAKEVIEW
FRESNO
LOS ANGELES
FREEL PEAK
BLUE LAKE
O'MALLEY
MARTIN
FOUNTAIN
SIERRA
LAKE TAHOE BLVD.
N
TAHOE KEYS BLVD.
VENICE DR.
TAHOE ISLAND
3RD ST.
2ND ST.
4TH ST.
DUNLAP
HIGHWAY 89
12TH ST.
15TH ST.
13TH ST.
JULIE
TATA
South Tahoe Y
C ST.
MELBA
HIGHWAY 50
TATA
B ST.
D ST.
City Services Center
LAKE TAHOE BLVD.

SEASONAL EVENTS

January. *South Lake Tahoe Winter Carnival.* At the Sierra Ski Ranch, usually during the last week of the month. Week-long event, featuring ski races, costume contests, dancing and entertainment, and a variety of other festivities. For more information, call the Sierra Ski Ranch at (916) 659-7453.

May.. *Great Lake Tahoe Sternwheeler Race.* Held during Memorial weekend. Popular annual event, featuring a boat race between Lake Tahoe's two famous paddlewheelers, the *M.S. Dixie* and *Tahoe Queen.* For more information, call (916) 544-5050 or the respective cruise boat operators.

June. *The Wagon Train Festival.* A wagon train comprising 30 authentic 19th century wagons rolls through town, along Highway 50, en route to Placerville. The wagons make an overnight stop in South Lake Tahoe; celebrations include street dancing and other festivities. For a schedule and information, call (916) 626-2344.

July. *Star Spangled Fourth,* South Lake Tahoe. Firework displays, acrobatic air show and a variety of Independence Day celebrations. For more information, call the South Lake Tahoe Chamber of Commerce; (916) 541-5255. *Lake Tahoe Sail Week.* Usually held at the end of the month. Week-long event featuring sailboat racing; national championship competitions. (916) 541-0176. *Sierra Nevada Open Golf Tournament.* Held at the Edgewood Golf Course, Stateline. Long-running, annual Pro-Am invitational tournament. For exact dates, call the South Lake Tahoe Visitors Bureau at (916) 544- 5050.

August. *Amacker Ranch Rodeo.* Hosted by the Amacker Ranch at Tahoe Paradise, just south of South Lake Tahoe. One of the best-known rodeos in the area; annual event. For a schedule, call the Visitors Bureau at (916) 544-5050.

September. *World's Toughest Triathlon,* South Lake Tahoe. Prestigious one-day event, featuring some of the world's top athletes. Individual and team competition; gruelling 148.6-mile course. For more information, call (916) 544-5050.

December. If you are in the area on New Year's Eve, don't miss the *Torchlight Parade* at Kirkwood Ski Resort, nor the elaborate celebrations at the Stateline, South Lake Tahoe.

TOURS

Scenic Tours

Grayline has coach tours of Lake Tahoe and historic Virginia City, May-Sept. The Rim of the Lake Tour, which will show you around the entire lake, including on its route the fabled Ponderosa Ranch, lasts 4 hours and costs $20.00 per person; the Virginia City Tour costs $19.00, and takes 5 hours. For reservations and more information, call (702) 588-6688.

Scenic Flights

Sky Trek Aviation offers scenic flights over the Lake and the Sierra; flights originate at the Lake Tahoe Airport. For more information, call (916) 541-5500.

PLACES OF INTEREST

Historical Society Museum. 3058 Lake Tahoe Blvd. (Hwy. 50), South Lake Tahoe. Artifacts from Lake Valley's early days, some of Indian origin; also several old photographs depicting Lake Tahoe's history. Worth viewing too is a 1920s bobsled and two or three pieces of 19th-century farm machinery. Open Tues.-Sat. 11-4.

Heavenly Valley Aerial Tram. Located at Heavenly's California Base Lodge (follow signs from Ski Run Blvd., south off Hwy. 50, to the ski resort). A 50-passenger tram car takes you to the *Top of the Tram* restaurant, some 2,000 feet above lake level, offering spectacular views of the lake and surrounding mountains. The tram operates year-round. Also visit the ski area, "America's largest alpine ski resort," sprawled over 20 square miles, nine mountains and two states.

Casino District. At the Stateline, on the Nevada side. A half-mile glitter strip, this is home to some of Tahoe's finest hotel-casinos, including *Harrah's, Harvey's, Caesar's* and the *High Sierra*. Here is to be found non-stop gambling action and some of the best in big name entertainment. The district is an absolute must for visitors to the area.

Kingsbury Grade. Southeast of the Stateline casinos, off Hwy. 50; the grade actually forms part of Nevada Route 207. Drive up the grade to Daggett Summit (elev. 7,375 feet), then down the Haines Canyon in a more less vertical drop, and into the Carson Valley; the descent is approximately 3,000 feet, achieved in just over 6 miles. This is one of the most spectacular drives at the lake, with great views of both the Carson Valley and Lake Tahoe.

Zephyr Cove. 4 miles north of Stateline, on Hwy.50 east. Well-liked summer resort, with a marina, a sandy beach, and stables. Also home port of *M.S. Dixie*, a glass-bottomed Mississippi river boat, Lake Tahoe's oldest cruise boat. The resort is open May-Oct.

Historic Tallac Estates. Situated between Camp Richardson and *Kiva Beach Recreation Area*, off Hwy. 89; reached via Kiva Beach Rd. Park at Kiva and explore on foot. Tour some splendid 1920s homes, including the *Pope-Tevis Estate*, the *McGonagles Estate*, and the *Baldwin Estate*. Visit also the *Tallac Museum* and *Tallac* site. Open June-Sept.

Visitors Center. Also off Hwy. 89; look for the turnoff 300 feet past Kiva Beach turnoff. Visit the *Stream Profile Chamber*, an enclosed viewing area at stream level, which shows off native fish in their natural habitat; in the fall, you can watch giant Kokanee Salmon as they swim upstream. Some worthwhile walking trails can also be enjoyed here, starting out from near the center. Open June-Sept.

Emerald Bay State Park. Approximately 8 miles north of South Lake Tahoe, on Hwy. 89. The park contains in it the magnificent Emerald Bay, billed as "the most beautiful inland harbor in the world." Also splendid walking trails, campgrounds, picnic areas and waterfalls. A highlight of the park is the fabled *Vikingsholm*, situated in the cradle of the bay, and reached by way of a mile-long hike from the parking area on the northwest corner. *Vikingsholm* is a masterful replica of a 1,200-year-old Viking castle, acknowledged as "the finest example of Scandinavian architecture in North America." Tours of the 38-room castle are conducted by State Park personnel in summer. Some lovely Scandinavian antiques and furniture can be viewed within, as well as Norwegian weavings, a Swedish wood-carving, and several ornate fixtures. Open July-Aug. 10-4.

Fallen Leaf Lake. A self-contained summer resort, 5 miles west of South Tahoe; reached via Fallen Leaf Road, the turnoff for which lies just past Camp Richardson, off Hwy. 89. View Fallen Leaf Lodge, built in 1913. Opportunities for camping, hiking, fishing, boating and horseback riding. Open May-Sept.

Friday's Station. Corner of Hwy. 50 and Loop Road, set slightly back from the highway. Charming, beautifully restored Bonanza era hostelry and Pony Express remount station, originally built in 1860. A private residence now; view from highway.

Cave Rock. 2 miles north of Zephyr Cove, on Hwy. 50. Ancient Tahoe landmark, comprising a volcanic neck formed nearly 5 million years ago. Features two tunnels, and a small rest area directly below, with good fishing possibilities.

Art Galleries. *Allen Augustine Gallery*, located in the Round Hill Mall, Zephyr Cove (702) 588-3525; features original paintings and sculptures. *Sierra Galleries*, at Caesar's Tahoe Hotel-Casino, Stateline, (702) 588-8500; bronze sculptures, and paintings. *DeCurtis Art Gallery*, (702) 588-7310; located in the Round Hill Village, Round Hill.

LAKE CRUISES

One of the most enjoyable ways of seeing the lake is on board a cruise boat. South Lake Tahoe has two of the largest cruise boats at the lake, and one or two smaller craft, all offering scheduled Emerald Bay Cruises, Sunset Dinner and Dance Cruises, and a host of other cruises of varying lengths and descriptions.

Tahoe Queen. Berthed at the Ski Run Marina in South Lake Tahoe, at the bottom end of Ski Run Boulevard. The *Tahoe Queen* is a large, 500-passenger, glass-bottomed Mississippi-riverboat-type paddlewheeler, operated by *Lake Tahoe Cruises*. It offers a variety of cruises daily, with live commendary and music on most. Cost for an *Emerald Bay Cruise* is $12.50 adults and $4.50 children; the *Sunset Dinner and Dance Cruise* is $34.00-$36.00 (dinner included). *Lake Tahoe Cruises* also offers charters for groups, parties, weddings and other occasions, as well as a *Squaw Valley Shuttle* ($16.50 round trip). For more information, call (916) 541-3364 or (916) 541-4652.

M.S. Dixie. Berthed at the Zephyr Cove Marina, 4 miles north of the Stateline on Highway 50. A 350-passenger, glass-bottomed Mississippi-riverboat-type sternwheeler, the *M.S. Dixie* is Lake Tahoe's oldest cruise boat in operation, which made its debut on the lake in 1947. It offers a variety of lake cruises, most of them daily, May-Oct. Cost: *Emerald Bay Cruise*, $12.00 adults and $4.00 children; *Sunset Dinner and Dance Cruise*, $29.50 (dinner included). Other cruises include the *South Shore Cruise* and the *Champagne Brunch Cruise*. Also available are charters for private parties, weddings and other special occasions. For information and reservations, call (702) 588-3508/(702) 882-0786.

Woodwind. Also berthed at the Zephyr Cove Marina, 4 miles north of the Stateline. The *Woodwind* is a trimaran, and one of the largest sailing vessels at the lake. It offers lake cruises during summer, May-Oct., sailing quite randomly into the sunsets. Cost for the *Day Cruises* is $10.00 adults and $4.50 children; and for the *Sunset Champagne Cruises*, $16.00 adults. Private charters are also available for weddings and parties. For reservations and more information, call (702) 588-3000.

FISHING

(A valid California or Nevada fishing license is required to fish in the Tahoe area lakes and streams. For a license and local fishing regulations, contact the *Department of Fish and Game*, Box 10678, Reno, Nevada; (702) 784-6214; or Box 72, Tahoe City, California; (916) 583-3325.)

Fishing Hot Spots

Rubicon Point. Off the northern tip of the D.L. Bliss State Park, extending nearly a mile south; Kokanee salmon are plentiful at depths of 80 feet (June-September).

Emerald Point. At the mouth of Emerald Bay, close into the shore, toplining is favored for Rainbows and Browns.

Southwest Corner. A mile out from the Baldwin and Kiva beaches, Kokanee are plentiful; and just east of there, inshore fishing is promising.

Buoy Run. Out from the Al Tahoe shoreline, deepline fishing at depths of 60-200 feet is suggested.

Ski Run. Just north from the Bijou shore, deepline at depths of 100-400 feet.

Hobart Hole. Opposite Nevada Beach, just south of Elk Point; excellent Mackinaw at depths of around 60 feet.

Zephyr Cove Run. In the Zephyr Cove area; deepline at depths of 100-400 feet.

East Shore. From Cave Rock north to nearly Glenbrook Bay; inshore fishing is excellent, some of the best at the lake.

Desolation Wilderness Lakes. Most of the area's 80 lakes are blessed with Brooks, Browns, Goldens and Rainbows.

Fallen Leaf Lake. Browns, Mackinaw, Rainbows, and Kokanee are abundant.

Lower Echo Lake. Rainbow trout and Kokanee salmon remain native to this lake.

Fishing Guides

Year-round fishing charters and guide services are available at *Tahoe Keys Sportfishing*, South Lake Tahoe (916-541-3131); *O'Malley's Fishing Charters*, Zephyr Cove (702-588-4102); *Bruce Hernandez*, South Tahoe (916-577-2246); *Dennis' Fishing Charters*, South Tahoe (916-577-6834); *Tahoe Sports Fishing*, South Tahoe (916-541-5448).

HIKING TRAILS

(Wilderness Permits are required for some of the trails. For a permit, maps and additional information, contact the *Lake Tahoe Basin Management Unit*, South Lake Tahoe (916 573-2600); or, *El Dorado National Forest Information Center*, Pollock Pines (916 644-6048).

Emerald Bay Area

Eagle Falls Trail. From the Eagle Falls Picnic Area, a steep climb leads into the Desolation Wilderness, with Eagle Lake being reached at the end of it; beautiful views of the basin are afforded enroute. 2-mile round trip, taking approximately 1½ hours.

Bayview Trail. Also a steep trail, it begins at the back of the Bayview Picnic Area. The trail offers some spectacular views of Lake Tahoe. 2-mile round trip; allow 2 hours.

Vikingsholm Trail. From the parking area just north of Eagle Falls, the trail descends into the cradle of Emerald Bay, leading to the fabled Vikingsholm Castle built by Mrs. Lora Knight in 1929; the castle is open to public between 10 a.m. and 4 p.m., May-Sept. 1 mile, 1 hour each way.

Rubicon Trail. The trail starts out at Vikingsholm Castle in Emerald Bay and traces the periphery of the lake to a point at the north end of the D.L. Bliss State Park. 4½-mile trail; allow a full day.

Balancing Rock and Lighthouse Trails. Both trails are short, self-guided trails through the northern part of the D.L. Bliss State Park. The first, a ½-mile trail, leads to the Balancing Rock; the other takes you on a ¾-mile walk to the site of an old lighthouse above Rubicon Point.

Visitors Center Area

Washoe Trail. This short trail begins at the end of the Visitors Center parking lot, and is especially interesting as it depicts the lifestyle and survival methods of Washoe Indians. Allow 30 minutes for the walk.

Taylor Creek Trail. This trail begins on the Washoe Trail, then branches off and follows alongside Taylor Creek to the north shore of Fallen Leaf Lake. ¾ mile, 30 minutes.

Lake of the Sky Trail. From the back of the Visitors Center, the trail winds past a small amphitheather and down to the Lake Tahoe shoreline. ¼ mile, 15 minutes.

Fallen Leaf Lake Area

Floating Island Trail. A sign-posted trailhead is situated ½ mile in from Highway 89, on Spring Creek Road. The trail follows the eastern slopes of Mount Tallac to Floating Island Lake, where the site of a real floating island can be seen. 2-mile trail, allow 1½ hours.

Angora Lakes Trail. From the end of Angora Lakes Road, south of Fallen Leaf Lake, a short, uphill, wooded trail leads to the twin Angora Lakes; swimming and fishing are possible at the lakes. ½-mile trail; 20 minutes.

Frederick's Trail. Starting out at Fallen Leaf Road, ¼ mile south of the Fallen Leaf Campground, the trail leisurely loops around a meadow. 1¼-mile loop, allow 1½ hours.

Grass Lake Trail. From Fallen Leaf Lake drive down Glen Alpine Road to Lily Lake; the trail begins at Lily Lake and winds past the Glen Alpine Springs to Grass Lake, which is situated inside the Desolation Wilderness area. 2 miles of trail; 1½ hours.

Gilmore Lake Trail. Follow the Grass Lake trail to Glen Alpine Springs, then branch off along the northwest trail; a modest climb leads to Gilmore Lake at the base of Mount Tallac. Allow a full day for this 4-mile hike.

Susie Lake/Heather Lake Trail. This trail is also accessed from the Grass Lake trailhead. The trail leads past Glen Alpine Springs and through 4 miles of rugged country to Susie Lake, which is situated in the wilderness, continuing another mile to Heather Lake. Allow a full day.

Mount Tallac Trail. There are two different approaches to the summit: one by way of Glen Alpine Springs, and the other via the Floating Island. The Glen Alpine Springs route is 6 miles long, with a gradual climb, while the Floating

Island route is only 4 miles, but considerably steeper. Either way, allow a full day for a hike to the summit.

Echo Lakes Area

Echo Lakes Trail. Skirting both Upper and Lower Echo lakes is a 2-mile trail that takes approximately 1½ hours to complete. A boat hire is also available between the two lakes. Parking is available at Lower Echo Lake, at the end of Echo Lakes Road.

Tamarack Lake Trail. Follow the Echo Lakes Trail a mile past Upper Echo Lake to Tamarack Lake. It is a 3-mile trail that can be reduced to a third of its length by use of a boat across the two Echo Lakes.

Lake Aloha Trail. Again, follow the Echo Lakes trail, first to Tamarack Lake, then 3 miles farther to the man-made Lake Aloha—one of the largest lakes in the Desolation Wilderness area. 6 miles each way; allow a full day.

Hawley Grade Trail. From Echo Summit this trail descends to the Upper Truckee River, offering magnificent views of South Lake Tahoe. Originally a wagon road, built in 1854 by one Asa H. Hawley, this trail once represented the first "reasonable descent" into Lake Valley. The trail is 2½ miles long, and takes just over 2 hours to complete.

Meiss Lake Country. Situated some 6 miles south of Tahoe Paradise (Meyers), this trail system comprises several miles of trails and lakes. A sign-posted trailhead is located roughly 5 miles south of Highway 50, leading to trails of varying lengths and descriptions.

BICYCLING

There are many miles of bike trails to be enjoyed on the south shore of Lake Tahoe. Bike rentals are available at several locations throughout South Lake Tahoe, including two or three outdoor lots along Emerald Bay Road, just to the north of the South Tahoe Y.

Bike rentals in the city area are available at *TahoeBike Shop,* 2277 Highway 50, (916) 544-8060; *Tahoe Cyclery,* 3552 Lake Tahoe Blvd., (916) 541-2726; *Sierra Cycle Works,* 3430 Highway 50, (916) 541-7505; *Lakeview Sports,* 3131 Highway 50, (916) 544-7160; *Anderson's Bicycle Rental,* 645 Emerald Bay Road, (916) 541-0500; and *The Outdoorsman Bike Shop*, 2358 Highway 50, (916) 541-1660.

BEACHES AND PICNIC AREAS

Beaches

Baldwin Beach. Off Highway 89, 1½ miles northwest of Camp Richardson. Facilities include picnic area, swimming area, fire pits, restrooms and parking; no dogs or boats are permitted on the beach.

Kiva Beach. Just north of Visitors Center, with the forest bordering on it; sign-posted turn-off. Picnic areas, fire pits, restrooms, and parking.

Pope Beach. A mile east of Kiva Beach; access via Pope Beach Road, just east of Camp Richardson. Picnic area, fire pits, and restrooms and parking facilities; no dogs or boats.

Barton Beach. Between Tahoe Keys and Lakeview Avenue (east of Tahoe Keys). This is one of the smaller beaches in the area, accessible only by boat. Facilities are limited to restrooms, swimming area and a lifeguard; boats are permitted, except in the marked swimming area.

Regan Beach. Located at the foot of Sacramento Avenue, just over Lakeview Avenue, in Al Tahoe. Picnic area, swimming area, grass area, restrooms, parking, concession stand, play equipment, wind-surfing rentals, and on-duty lifeguard (summers only between 11 a.m. and 6 p.m.). No dogs, fires, or alcohol permitted on beach.

El Dorado Beach. Almost adjacent to Regan Beach, abutting Lake Tahoe Boulevard (Highway 50) across from the City Campground and the South Lake Tahoe Chamber of Commerce. Picnic area, swimming area, lifeguard, boat ramp, parking, and restrooms.

Connolly Beach. Behind the Timber Cove Lodge, at the end of Bal Bijou Road. Swimming area, lifeguard, concession stand, restrooms, and limited parking.

Nevada Beach. Off Highway 50, south of Elk Point (near Round Hill). Picnic area, swimming area, fire pits, and restroom and parking facilities.

Zephyr Cove. North of Round Hill, off Highway 50. Boat ramp, boat rentals, picnic area, fire pits, and restroom and parking facilities.

Picnic Areas

Truckee River Park. Off Highway 50, just over the Upper Truckee River (adjacent to Carrows Restaurant). Picnic tables, and fishing; no other facilities.

Taylor Creek. At the mouth of the creek; approach via trail from the Visitors Center. No facilities apart from those available at the Visitors Center.

Fallen Leaf Lake. At the southern end of the lake; take Fallen Leaf Road off Highway 89 and follow south. In addition to a picnic area, the Fallen Leaf Lake recreation area also has a small beach, restrooms, a general store and a marina.

Bayview Picnic Area. Just off Highway 89, at the southwest corner of Emerald Bay. Facilities include picnic tables, fire pits and restrooms.

Inspiration Point. On Highway 89, above the Bayview Picnic Area. Picnicking, and restrooms.

Eagle Falls. On Highway 89, at the head of Emerald Bay. Picnic area, fire pits, restrooms.

Emerald Bay Picnic Area. Near Vikingsholm, on the shores of Emerald Bay. Small beach area, picnicking, and restrooms; camping available in summer. Parking is off Highway 89.

CAMPGROUNDS

Emerald Bay Boat Campground. On the north shore of Emerald Bay, with access by boat or foot only; (916) 541-3030. 20 sites, restrooms, swimming and fishing; 10-day limit.

Eagle Point Campground. Near the mouth of Emerald Bay, on the southeast corner (entrance off Highway 89, 4½ miles northwest of Camp Richardson); (916) 541-3030. 100 sites, restrooms, showers, swimming, hiking and fishing; 10-day limit.

Fallen Leaf Campground. Just north of Fallen Leaf Lake, ½ mile in from Highway 89; (916) 544-0426. 205 sites, restrooms, swimming, fishing, hiking and riding; 7-day limit.

Camp Richardson. On Highway 89, 1½ miles northwest of South Lake Tahoe; (916) 541-1801. 230 sites, restrooms, showers, electrical hook-ups, store, laundromat, marina and stables. No day limit.

Tahoe Valley Campground. Off Highway 50, just west of the South Tahoe Y; (916) 541-2222. 300 sites, restrooms, showers, electrical hook-ups, store, hiking; no day limit.

Tahoe Pines Campground. On Highway 50, in Tahoe Paradise; (916) 577-1653. 60 sites, restrooms, showers, electrical hook-ups, hiking, riding and fishing; no day limit. Open year-round.

KOA Campground. Highway 50, Tahoe Paradise; (916) 577-3693. 20 sites, restrooms, showers, electrical hook-ups, store, laundromat, swimming, hiking, riding and fishing; no day limit. Open year-round.

El Dorado Campground. Situated in the city area, at the corner of Rufus Allen and Lake Tahoe Boulevard (Highway 50); (916) 544-3317. 166 sites, restrooms, showers, electrical hook-ups, boat ramp, recreation and beach area, swimming and fishing; 15-day limit.

Nevada Beach Campground. Off Highway 50 east, 1 mile north of the Stateline casinos; (916) 573-2600. 54 sites, restrooms, store, laundromat, swimming and fishing, handicapped access; 7-day limit.

Zephyr Cove Resort Campground. Highway 50 east, 4 miles north of the Stateline; (702) 588-6644. 170 sites, restrooms, showers, electrical hook-ups, boat ramp, store, laundromat, beach area, swimming and fishing; 14-day limit. Open all year.

Outlying Area Campgrounds. The following are mostly out-of-area camp-grounds, situated 8-10 miles south of Tahoe Paradise: *Crystal Springs,* 21 sites, (702) 882-2766; *Hope Valley,* 20 sites, (702) 882-2766; *Kit Carson,* 12 sites, (702) 882-2766; *Snowshoe Springs,* 13 sites, (702) 882-2766; *Grover Hot Springs,* 76 sites, (916) 694-2248; *Indian Creek Reservoir,* 29 sites, (702) 882-1631; and *Markleeville Campground,* 10 sites, (702) 882-2766.

WATER SPORTS

Marinas

Richardson's Marina. Off Highway 89, on Jameson Beach Road, Camp Richardson; (916) 541-1777. Facilities available: buoys, ramp, hoist, rentals, gas supplies, and repair service. Open all year.

Tahoe Keys Marina. Off Tahoe Keys Boulevard, on Venice Drive, Tahoe Keys; (916) 541-2155. 150 slips, ramp, forklift launching, rentals, gas supplies, repair service, sales and storage. Open year-round.

Timber Cove Marina. Off Highway 50, on Wagon Road, Bijou (behind Timber Cove Lodge); (916) 544-2942. Buoys, hoist, rentals, gas supplies, repair service, and sales. Open through summer.

Ski Run Marina. At the lake's end of Ski Run Boulevard, in the city; (916) 544-0200. 35 slips, buoys, ramp, gas supplies, repairs, rentals, sales, beach and snack bar. Open summers.

Lakeside Marina. At the bottom of Park Avenue, near Stateline; (916) 541-6626. 94 slips, buoys, ramp, gas supplies, rentals, sales and storage. Open summers.

Zephyr Cove Marina. Off Highway 50 east, 4 miles north of the Stateline; (702) 588-3833. Buoys, ramp, rentals, supplies, and restaurant. Open through summer.

Public Launching Ramps. There are five public boat-launching ramps in the area—at *El Dorado Beach*, in the city area; at *Zephyr Cove*, 4 miles north of Stateline; at *Cave Rock*, 3 miles north of Zephyr Cove; at *Logan Shoals*, 1½ miles north of Cave Rock (just off Highway 50); and at *Glenbrook*, another 4 miles farther north of Cave Rock.

Water Skiing

Lake Tahoe Water Ski School. At Round Hill Pines Beach, Round Hill; (916) 573-0603. Lessons and equipment rentals; also sailboarding.

Werley's Water Ski School. Timber Cove Pier, South Lake Tahoe; (916) 544-5099. Lessons, equipment rentals, and ski tows.

Jet Ski Rentals

Lakeview Sports. 3131 Highway 50 (across from El Dorado Campground), South Lake Tahoe; (916) 544-7160. Jet ski and windsurfer rentals.

Ski Run Boat Rentals. Ski Run Marina, South Lake Tahoe; (916) 544-0200. Jet ski rentals; also power boat rentals and parasail rides.

Watersports of Tahoe. Two locations, at the Timber Cove Pier, (916) 544-5387, and at Camp Richardson, (916) 541-4386. Jet skis and waverunners.

Zephyr Cove Resort. Highway 50, Zephyr Cove; (702) 588-3833. Jet sis, power boats, paddle boats; also waterskiing.

GOLF

Tahoe Paradise Golf Course. Off Highway 50, 4 miles south of the Y; (916) 577-2121. 18 holes, 4119 yards, 66 Par; green fee: $19.50/18 Holes, $12.00/9 Holes. Facilities: Carts, pro shop, driving range, coffee shop.

Lake Tahoe Country Club. 1 mile south of the Lake Tahoe Airport, on Highway 50; (916) 577-0788. 18 holes, 6588 yards, 71 Par; green fee: $25.00/18 Holes, $15.00 twilight. Carts, pro shop, driving range, cocktail lounge and snack bar.

Bijou Golf Course. Wedged between Johnson Boulevard and Fairway Avenue, in the city; (916) 544-5500. 9 holes, 2015 yards, 33 Par; green fee: $5.00/9 holes. Carts.

Edgewood Tahoe Golf Club. On Loop Road, behind the High Sierra Hotel-Casino; (702) 588-3566. 18 holes, 7563 yard championship course, 72 Par; green fee: $100.00/with cart (cart mandatory). Pro shop, driving range, restaurant, bar.

Glenbrook Golf Course. On the east shore, 8 miles north of the Stateline; (702) 749-5201. 9 holes, 2591 yards, 34 Par. green fee: $27.00/all day, $20.00/twilight. Carts, pro shop, driving range, bar and snack bar.

TENNIS

South Tahoe High School. Lake Tahoe Boulevard, 1 mile west of the Tahoe Valley Y; (916) 541-4611. 6 courts, lights.

South Tahoe Intermediate School. Lyons Avenue, off Lake Tahoe Boulevard (Highway 50); (916) 541-4611. 8 courts, lights.

George Whittle High School. Warrior Way, Zephyr Cove (off Highway 50 east); (702) 588-3666. 4 courts, lights.

HORSEBACK RIDING

Camp Richardson Corral, 2 miles northwest of the Tahoe Valley Y, on Emerald Bay Road, (916) 541-3113; breakfast and dinner rides, guided trail rides, fishing and pack trips, wagon and sleigh rides.

Cascade Stables, 1 mile past Camp Richardson, also on Emerald Bay Road, (916) 541-2055; guided trail rides, breakfast and dinner rides, fishing, hunting and pack trips.

Stateline Stables, Park Avenue (behind the Crescent V Shopping Center), next to the Stateline, (916) 541-0962; guided scenic trail rides.

Zephyr Cove Riding Stables, 4½ miles north of the Stateline casinos (at Zephyr Cove Resort), (702) 588-5664; guided trail rides, breakfast, lunch and dinner rides.

Sunset Ranch, Hwy. 50, ¼ mile west of the airport, South Lake Tahoe, (916) 541-9001; guided and unguided trail rides, hay rides, dinner rides. Open year round.

WINTER SPORTS

Downhill Ski Areas

Heavenly Valley. This 20-square-mile expanse, America's largest alpine ski area, straddles the California-Nevada stateline a couple of miles to the south of South Lake Tahoe's "casino district"; West Heavenly lies in California, and Heavenly North in Nevada. In California, approach via Ski Run Boulevard, off Highway 50; in Nevada, Benjamin Drive, off the Kingsbury Grade, leads straight to the base of the mountain. Heavenly's elevations: top 10,167 feet, base 6,100 feet; vertical drop 3,600 feet. Facilities available: 26 lifts, helicopter skiing, NASTAR races, lessons, rentals, restaurant and bar, and shuttle bus. Lift prices: $35.00/adults, $14.00/children; half day: $23.00 adults, $14.00/children. Phone (916) 541-1330.

Kirkwood Ski Resort. Take Highway 89 south to Pickett's Junction; at the junction take Highway 88 west to Kirkwood. Although slight of the way, this ski area enjoys some of the heaviest snowfall in the region, and remains open through to the Fourth of July. Elevations: top 9,800 feet, base 7,800 feet; vertical

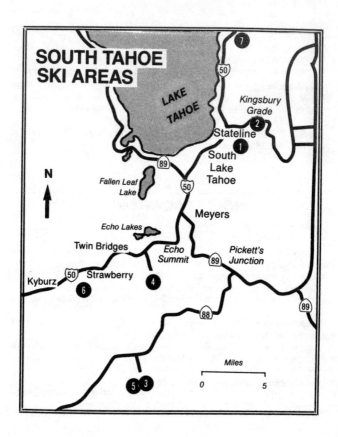

Downhill Ski Areas -
1) Heavenly Valley West
2) Heavenly Valley North
3) Kirkwood Ski Resort
4) Sierra Ski Ranch

Nordic Ski Areas -
5) Kirkwood Touring Center
6) Strawberry Ski Touring
7) Spooner Summit Nordic (Wilderness) Ski Area

drop 2,000 feet. Facilities include 11 lifts, NASTAR races, lessons, rentals, bar, snack bar, restaurant, store, and shuttle bus. Lift prices: $33.00/adults, $15.00/children; half day: $24.00/adults, $10.00/children. Phone (209) 258-7247.

Sierra Ski Ranch. Just off Highway 50, 12½ miles southwest of South Lake Tahoe. Elevations: top 8,852 feet, base 6,640 feet; vertical drop 2,212 feet. Facilities: 9 lifts, lessons, rentals, day lodges, snack bar, mountain top restaurant, and shuttle bus. Lift prices: $27.00/adults, $13.00/children; half day: $20.00/adults, $10.00/children. Phone (916) 659-7453.

Nordic Ski Areas

Kirkwood Touring Center. At the Kirkwood Ski Area on Highway 88, 28 miles south of South Lake Tahoe. 75 miles of trails; tours, lessons, rentals, restaurant, lodge, child care, and shuttle bus. Trail fee: $12.00. Phone (209) 258-7248.

Strawberry Ski Touring. 14 miles from South Lake Tahoe on Highway 50 at Kyburz. 12 miles of trails; lessons, rentals, lodge. No trail fee. Phone (916) 659-7585.

Wilderness Cross-Country Ski Areas

Angora Ridge Area. Approach via Lake Tahoe Boulevard (west of the "Y") and Tahoe Mountain Road; the trailhead is situated just past Glenmore Way and Dundee Circle.

Tahoe Paradise Area. From Highway 50 (in the Tahoe Paradise area) turn into Pioneer Trail, then continue on down, about a mile, to Oneidas Street. The trailhead is just south of Oneidas, off Chibcha Street.

High Meadows Area. Take Pioneer Trail to High Meadows Trail, just south of Lake Christopher. Follow High Meadows Trail to the trailhead.

Toiyabe National Forest Area. Take the Kingsbury Grade (Route 207) to North Benjamin Drive, then follow North Benjamin to Andria Drive; the trailhead is located at the end of Andria Drive.

Spooner Summit Area. The trailhead is located near Spooner Summit, just east of the junction of Highways 50 and 28.

Snowmobiling

There are two locations, both in the Tahoe Paradise area, where groomed tracks are available for snowmobiling: *Lake Tahoe Winter Sports Center,* (916) 577-2940; and *Tahoe Paradise Winter Sports* (916) 577-9579. Guided backcountry tours are also offered by *Snowmobilin' Adventures,* (702) 588-3833.

Snow Play Areas

There are two snow play areas in the South Lake Tahoe area. The first is located just north of Taylor Creek, off Highway 89; the other, *Hansen's Resort,* (916) 544-3361, is situated off Ski Run Boulevard in the city. Hansen's offers on-site equipment, banked turns and packed runs, mechanical lift returns, and even lodging on the premises.

RESTAURANTS

(Restaurant prices—based on full course dinner, excluding drinks, tax and tips—are categorized as follows: *Deluxe*, over $30; *Expensive*, $20-$30; *Moderate*, $10-$20; *Inexpensive*, under $10.)

The Beacon. *Expensive.* Hwy. 89, Camp Richardson; (916) 541-0630. Beachfront restaurant, serving primarily seafood and continental dishes. Live jazz music. Lunch and dinner; brunch on weekends. Reservations advised.

The Broiler Room. *Expensive.* At Caesar's Tahoe Hotel-Casino; (702) 586-2025. Beef, lamb, and poultry dishes; also seafood, and Cajun specialties. Open for dinner. Reservations recommended.

Cantina Los Tres Hombres. *Inexpensive.* 765 Emerald Bay Rd.; (916) 544-1233. Authentic Mexican cooking. Cocktail lounge. Lunch and dinner daily.

Chez Villaret. *Expensive.* 900 Emerald Bay Rd.; (916) 541-7868. Acknowledged as one of South Lake Tahoe's finest French restaurants, featuring Nouvelle and Classic French cuisine. Award-winning wine list. Dinner daily; reservations recommended.

Christiania Inn. *Deluxe.* Across from Heavenly Valley ski area; (916) 544-7337. Delightful alpine inn, with large stone fireplace. Gourmet continental cuisine; creative desserts. Dining room featured in *Bon Appetit* magazine. Dinner daily; reservations required.

Cuckoo's Nest Cafe. *Expensive.* 2502 Highway 50, South Lake Tahoe; (916) 541-0873. European dishes, prepared with the freshest ingredients. Dinners from 6 p.m. Reservations advised.

The Dory's Oar. *Expensive.* 1041 Fremont Ave.; (916) 541-6603. Well-known seafood restaurant, established in 1975. House specialties include live Maine lobster and Maryland soft shell crabs. New England atmosphere. Open for dinner daily, lunch Mon.-Fri. Reservations recommended.

Eagle's Nest Inn. *Expensive.* 472 Needle Peak Rd., Stateline; (702) 588-6492/883-5225. Specializing in Italian and Continental cuisine. European atmosphere; views of Lake Tahoe. Open for breakfast, lunch and dinner daily. Reservations recommended.

El Dorado Buffet. *Moderate.* At the Harvey's Resort Hotel; (702) 588-2411. Great buffet luncheons, ideal for family dining. Breakfast, lunch and dinner daily.

El Vacquero. *Moderate.* At Harvey's Resort Hotel; (702) 588-2411. Mexican dishes; good selection. Open for lunch and dinner daily.

Empress Court. *Moderate.* At Caesar's Tahoe Hotel-Casino; (702) 588-3515. Specializing in Szechwan, Cantonese and Mandarin cuisine. Lunch and dinner daily.

Forest Restaurant. *Moderate.* At Harrah's Hotel-Casino; (702) 588-6606. Buffet-style restaurant. Casual atmosphere; panoramic mountain views. Open for breakfast, lunch and dinner, and Sunday brunch.

Fresh Ketch. *Expensive.* 2435 Venice Dr. East (at the Tahoe Keys Marina); (916) 541-5683. Spectacular views of the lake, and an enchanting waterfall featured inside the restaurant. Long Island oysters are the favorite here; also some poultry. Lunch and dinner daily; brunch on weekends. Reservations suggested.

Friday's Station. *Expensive.* At Harrah's, Stateline; (702) 588-6606. Notable Tahoe steakhouse, open for lunch and dinner daily.

The Hearthside. *Expensive.* At Tahoe Seasons Resort, Keller & Saddle Rds., Heavenly Valley; (916) 541-6700. Splendid mountain setting, across from the Heavenly Valley ski area. Menu features prime rib, steaks, seafood, pasta and veal. Also famous Mimosa brunch on Sundays, with champagne, cheeses, smoked salmon, omelettes, salads and pastries. Breakfast, lunch and dinner daily. Reservations recommended.

Le Posh. *Expensive-Deluxe.* At Caesar's Tahoe; (702) 588-3515. Elegant restaurant, featuring contemporary California cuisine. Extensive wine list. Reservations recommended.

Los Aguirres. *Inexpensive.* 2212 Lake Tahoe Boulevard, South Lake Tahoe; (916) 541-9849. Authentic Mexican food. Lunch and dinner daily.

Paul Kennedy's Steak House. *Moderate-Expensive.* 4114 Highway 50, South Lake Tahoe; (916) 541-5077. Popular steakhouse, located adjacent to Stateline casinos. Excellent selection of steaks; also fresh seafood. Extensive wine list. Open for dinner. Reservations suggested.

Primavera. *Expensive.* At Caesar's Tahoe; (702) 588-3515. Delightful poolside restaurant, specializing in Italian cuisine. House specialties include veal, calamari and linguini. Lunch and dinner daily; European-style brunch on weekends.

The Sage Room. *Expensive.* Housed in Harvey's Resort Hotel; (702) 588-2411. Exceptional dining, with several dishes prepared at the tableside. Steak specialties; Western atmosphere. Open for dinner daily; reservations required.

Stetson. *Deluxe.* At the High Sierra Hotel-Casino; (702) 588-6211. Mesquite-grilled steaks and seafood; elegant setting. Open for dinner; reservations recommended.

The Summit. *Deluxe.* At Harrah's Hotel-Casino; (702) 588-6606. Gourmet restaurant on 18th floor. Superb Continental cuisine. Live music. Spectacular views. Open for dinner. Reservations required.

Sushi House. *Moderate.* 3733 Highway 50, South Lake Tahoe; (916) 542-1242. Tempura, teriyaki, and full sushi bar. Lunch and dinner daily.

Swiss Chalet Restaurant. *Expensive.* Hwy. 50, 4 miles west of Stateline; (916) 544-3304. Owned and operated by the chef for over 30 years, the restaurant serves excellent steaks and European cuisine; also homemade Swiss pastries. Delightful alpine atmosphere. Cocktail lounge. Dinners daily; reservations recommended.

Tep's Villa Roma. *Moderate.* 3450 Hwy. 50; (916) 541-8227. Traditional Italian dishes, and freshly-baked Italian breads and garlic sticks. Also seafood specialties, and all-you-can-eat antipasto bar. Open for dinner daily.

Top of the Wheel. *Deluxe.* At Harvey's Resort Hotel; (702) 588-2411. Superb restaurant on the top floor of the hotel, with panoramic views of the lake and Sierras. Polynesian and American cuisine; live entertainment, dancing. Dinner daily; Sunday brunch. Reservations required.

The Waterwheel. *Moderate.* Crescent V Shopping Center, cnr. Hwy. 50 and Park Ave.; (916) 544-4158. Authentic Mandarin and Szechwan cuisine. Open for lunch and dinner.

Womack's Texas Style Bar-B-Que. *Moderate.* 1169 Ski Run Boulevard, South Lake Tahoe; (916) 541-9191. Open for breakfast, lunch and dinner.

Zachary's. *Expensive.* Behind Roundhill Mall, 2 miles north of Stateline; (702) 588-2108. Established, well-known restaurant, serving seafood, steak, chicken, veal and lamb. Also homemade desserts. Dinner from 6 p.m.; reservations recommended.

NORTH LAKE TAHOE

Wilderness and Summer Homes

North Lake Tahoe is a loosely defined, seasonally inhabited area, with roughly 40 miles of shoreline and completely surrounded by two of the most splendid forests—the Tahoe National Forest and the Toiyabe National Forest. There are at least one-half dozen state parks here as well, and several drives and walks through gorgeous, thickly-wooded back-country.

There are three broad geographic divisions of North Lake Tahoe: the West Shore, the North Shore, and the Tahoe-Truckee Route area (essentially the Truckee River Canyon area). The north and west shores are made up largely of tiny resort communities, dotted with hundreds of vacation homes, and with few year-round residents. Most of the permanent population of the area is concentrated mainly in four centers—Tahoe City, Kings Beach-Crystal Bay, Incline Village and Truckee—all of which are linked together via four or five state highways. Truckee, for instance, is linked to Tahoe City via Highway 89; Kings Beach and Crystal Bay are linked to Truckee by way of Highway 267; Incline Village, Kings Beach and Tahoe City are linked by Highway 28 (with Route 431 linking Incline to Highway 395 which leads to Reno); and the west shore communities are strung together and linked to Tahoe City by 89 south.

North Lake Tahoe is accessible by way of Interstate 80, which passes just over Truckee and intersects with a couple of the highways feeding into the North Tahoe area. There is also a non-commercial airport, the Tahoe-Truckee Airport, just to the southeast of Truckee.

Skiing at Royal Gorge, America's largest nordic ski resort

Sheltered cove near Sand Harbor, on the lake's east shore

THE TAHOE-TRUCKEE ROUTE

The Tahoe-Truckee Route comprises mainly the townships of Truckee and Tahoe City, lying some 15 miles apart, and the resort communities of Alpine Meadows and Squaw Valley which are just to the northwest of Tahoe City. The route follows the Truckee River through an ancient canyon formed thousands of years ago by an off-shoot glacier. It is especially picturesque in spring, when the river flows heartily, fuller with the snowmelt, its banks awash with light-green brush and a sprinkling of native wildflowers.

The Tahoe-Truckee Route is among the earliest incursions into North Lake Tahoe, dating from the late 1850's when the "Tahoe-Truckee Toll Road," a dusty, rutted turnpike, barely the width of a stagecoach, passed through the canyon. Several early day personages traveled by way of it, including Generals Ulysses S. Grant and Philip H. Sheridan, and the British royal mistress, Lily Langtree. In 1900 even a narrow-gauge railroad was pushed through the canyon, the first ever passenger train to enter the Lake Tahoe Basin; it provided rail service between Tahoe City and Truckee for over a quarter of a century.

Today the route continues to forge a vital link between two of North Tahoe's most important towns. The present highway (Highway 89), however, is cut at a slightly higher elevation than the original tollroad, but a bicycle path below the highway and closer to the river offers some unique opportunities and a slower pace by which to explore.

Truckee

The town of Truckee lies to the northwest of Tahoe City at the intersection of Interstate 80 and Highways 89 and 267, posing as both a crossroads and a "gateway" to North Lake Tahoe. Truckee is notable mostly for its abundance of historic buildings and sites, never more apparent than in its "historic downtown." Covered wooden walkways protrude from clapboard store-fronts, reminiscent of the Old West, and of some 300 buildings nestled there, nearly a third date from the 19th century and more than half from before World War II. Most of the buildings, however, are currently in use, housing specialty shops, restaurants and hotels. On Commercial Row, Truckee's main street, one of the oldest buildings is the I.O.O.F. Hall which was built by the Oddfellows in 1871 and where the I.O.O.F. still occupies the upper floor, with a restaurant on the ground floor. A few doors down, outside Cabona's, a clothing store on Commercial Row, is a plaque commemorating an early day vigilante group, "the 601." On the south side of the street is to be found the Southern Pacific Railroad Depot, dating from 1896, an inerasible reminder of Truckee's humble beginnings as a railroad settlement. Farther along, a little way from the depot are the old Ice House and the Loading Dock, both charming 19th century

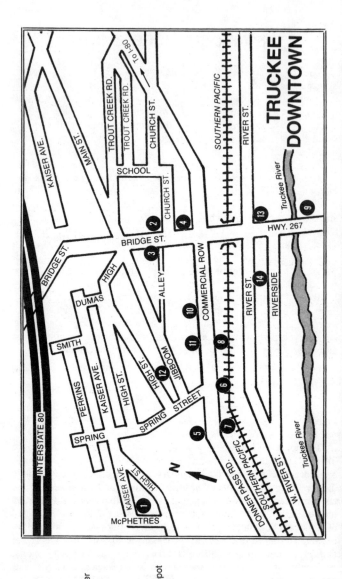

Points of Interest -
1) Rocking Stone Tower
2) Gray's Log Cabin
3) Alpenglow
4) Truckee Hotel
5) C.B. White's
6) Loading Dock
7) Ice House
8) Southern Pacific Depot
9) Chinese Herb Shop
10) I.O.O.F. Hall
11) The "601" Plaque
12) Truckee Jailhouse
13) River Street Cafe
14) Star Hotel

structures.

There are two Victorian buildings located on Commercial Row too: the C.B. White building, a Queen Anne Victorian with distinctive white-lace trim, built in 1874 by an early day lumber mill owner, W.H. Kruger, and later, in 1903, bought by an eminent banker, C.B. White, for whom it is named; and the Truckee Hotel (circa 1871), an unclassified Victorian, boasting 42 guest rooms decorated in 19th century splendor. The hotel, in fact, fronts on Bridge Street, and adjacent to it, just north on Church Street, is Truckee's oldest building, Gray's Log Cabin, built in 1863 by Joseph Gray, the town's first white settler. The cabin originally stood across the street from its present location, where the Alpenglow sports store now stands, but was moved in 1903. The stone structure of Alpenglow is also not without historic merit; it was built in 1907, as a carriage house and blacksmith shop.

Also of interest is Jibboom Street (which runs just to the back of Commercial Row), once the town's "red light district," sporting dozens of saloons and brothels. Upon it is now to be seen the old Truckee Jail, built in 1875 and said to be one of the West's oldest town jails; the jail was operative until 1964. Take the time also to drive up Spring Street, at the top end of which is to be found the Rocking Stone Tower where a 17-ton rock balances precariously on its natural rock pedestal, believed to be one of only 25 such rocks in the world. The "rocking stone" was recently cemented to its base to prevent any accidents, but even so its rocking motion has not been completely lost. Legend has it that the Washoe Indians used the rock's rocking motion to grind nuts and seeds in the early days.

Over the railroad tracks on the south side of Commercial Row, flanking Highway 267, are the River Street Cafe and the Star Hotel. The greystone building housing the cafe was erected in 1885 as a boarding house for lumberjacks and railroad and ice workers, and the hotel was built in 1869, also as a boarding house, by George Schaffer, contemporary and partner of Joseph Gray. Just south of the River Street Cafe is the old Chinese Herb Shop, a brick building with double iron doors, built in 1878. This is especially interesting for it is perhaps the last reminder of Truckee's once thriving Chinese community of some 10,000 strong. Truckee's Chinatown, in fact, was the second largest in the West during the 1860's and the only one of its kind in the High Sierra. But racial hatred plagued the Chinese, and by 1886 not a single Chinese remained in Truckee. The legacy of the Chinese, however, lingers to this day, for they, more than anyone else, had provided the labor for the building of the Central Pacific Railroad over the Sierra.

South on Highway 267 lies Martis Valley, with a lake of the same name nearby. In the valley are to be found the Tahoe-Truckee Airport, North Tahoe's only airport, and an elaborate sewage plant, billed as "the most modern tertiary plant in the world," through which the Tahoe-Truckee Sanitation Agency conducts tours year round. At the airport there are a couple of local aviation companies offering scenic flights over the lake, and in June the Truckee Airshow gets underway here, providing for some thrilling aerobatics and displays of vintage airplanes. In winter, usually in February, the airport also hosts the annual Sled Dog Races.

Four miles to the west of Truckee's downtown, on Donner Pass Road, which is really an extension of Commercial Row, one arrives at the Donner Memorial State Park, named for the ill-fated Donner Party who camped here during the fateful winter of 1846-47. According to history, the emigrant party led by George Donner became lost in these parts while attempting to cross over the Sierra. The party was ill-prepared for the bitter conditions they encountered, and eventually food in the camp ran out. Several members of the party perished as hunger and the cold gripped them, and the survivors resorted to cannibalism to stay alive until they were found by a rescue party the following spring. Of the original party of 89, 42 perished. In the park stands a monument, the Emigrant Monument, commemorating the tragedy; the statue of a "Donner family" stands atop a 22-foot-high pedestal, the height of the pedestal ironically indicating the depth of the snow during that perilous winter. Nearby, the one and one-half mile long and half-mile wide Donner Lake, too, is named for the party. There is an Emigrant Museum not far from the monument, displaying several artifacts and old photographs recounting the Donner Party story and the Central Pacific Railroad days. A sports museum, the Western American Ski Sport Museum, is located farther on at Soda Springs, accessible from I-80; it has several excellent exhibits of early day skis, some of them dating from 1860, as well as some Squaw Valley Winter Olympic Games memorabilia. Also to be recommended is a drive along the old Highway 40, which runs parallel to I-80; scenic views present themselves enroute, together with some rare glimpses of railroad "snow-sheds" constructed in the Central Pacific Railroad days, more than a century ago.

Truckee is also notable for its many lakes and reservoirs, among them Donner Lake and the Boca, Prosser and Stampede reservoirs. While producing excellent quantums of trout, these lakes and reservoirs are all the more interesting for their part in Truckee's ice industry, the most unusual industry the town has ever known. Between 1870 and 1927, ice was commercially harvested here and transported to far away markets on board the railroad, which by then had become central to Truckee's prosperity. Horses with spiked shoes were employed to drag across plows, skimming off snow from the ice, then cutters were drawn through the ice, again with the use of horses, to cut the ice into convenient slabs measuring 18 feet by 36 feet. The storage of the ice was a marvel in itself, with slabs stacked one on top of another, in rows alternately vertical and horizontal, and insulated with sawdust; it is told that when one such ice-storage unit burned down at the turn of the century, it took nearly three years for the ice in it to melt, so tightly was it packed.

Apart from the historic aspect, there is much else that Truckee boasts. It is, in fact, one of the fastest growing communities on the northern part of the lake today, with a host of modern shops, shopping centers, restaurants, lodging facilities, campgrounds, two golf courses, an elementary school, a high school, judicial courts, a local theater group, and even a local newspaper, the *Sierra Sun*. Coupled with this is the town's central location, only minutes away from several of North Lake Tahoe's ski areas, both alpine and nordic. Some local

events, such as the "Bath Tub Races" at Donner Lake and the Truckee
Rodeo at the Truckee River Park, add to the color. A striking fact about
this robust little town, however, is that it is known to record some of the
coldest temperatures in the state, but that, Truckee residents will tell
you, is an added attraction for most Californians who have known only
the sunny coastline. Indeed, here is a mountain town, at once historic
and vital, with Reno, "the Las Vegas of Northern Nevada," only 34
miles away.

South To Squaw Valley and Alpine Meadows

The drive south from Truckee on Highway 89 is most enchanting,
with the Truckee River flowing alongside of the road and lush pine
forests creeping up the granite walls of the canyon. Some 8 miles south,
on the east side of the highway, the twin peaks, Big Chief and Little
Chief (elevations 7232 and 7255 feet, respectively), come into view.
Big Chief is the more notable of the two, its west face vaguely
resembling the profile of an Indian Chief, for which it is named. And
like most other interesting-looking peaks and rocks in the region, this,
too, has been romanticized in a Washoe Indian legend which traces the
origins of the profile. According to the legend, there once dwelled an
Indian tribe just east of the peak here, and the chief of the tribe had a
beautiful daughter named Cedar Heart. The chief was overly protective
and even jealous of his daughter. He would not allow her to marry
among the tribe's braves, nor would he let her be seen with the young
warriors of the tribe. But one day, as the story goes, the chief found
Cedar Heart with a young brave named Ko-ta-ki. This enraged the chief
and he sought to have Ko-ta-ki put to death. But the couple fled, and the
chief assembled a war party and followed. The pursuit wound down to
the edge of the precipice where the Big Chief profile is now to be seen.
Here the young lovers saw the angry chief and his war party not far
behind, and they panicked; hand in hand they leaped to their deaths.
The chief, upon seeing what he had done, sank to the ground, his face in
the dirt, saddened, even deeply bereaved. Then a storm broke out,
lasting several hours. When finally the storm subsided, the chief tried
to rise but could not; his sorrow was too great, and the Great Spirit had
frozen his body to the ground. Thus the big chief remained, as the rain
and snow beat upon him, his body slowly disintegrating into the folds
of the earth—but his face became embedded in the rock, and there it
remains, looking out over what has come to be known as "Lover's
Leap."

Two miles to the southwest of Big Chief lies the famous Squaw
Valley, site of the VIII Winter Olympic Games in 1960. At the Squaw
Valley Road turnoff stands the Tower of Nations, with its five-ringed
Olympic insignia, and the Olympic flame flickering above it. At the far
end of the valley is the Olympic Village Inn, a lovely alpine-design

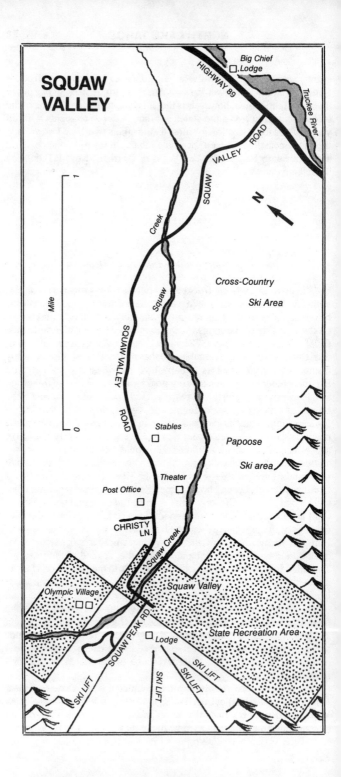

condominium complex, with one or two interesting restaurants, sprawled on the very site of the original Olympic Village where the athletes were housed and fed during the 1960 Games. Most of the other Olympic era facilities and landmarks, however, are now largely gone from the scene.

Squaw Valley itself is a natural amphitheater, surrounded by a series of noble mountain peaks, the highest of which, Granite Chief, soars 9050 feet, providing for some excellent skiing. The ski lodge area is nestled in the center of the bowl, with an aerial tram operating from the lodge to the Granite Chief restaurant, some 2000 feet above, with superb, all-round views of the valley to be enjoyed from there. Interestingly, the valley was the site of an elusive gold strike in the early 1860's, and later on a flourishing hay-farming community. It first opened to skiing in 1949, commanding the attention of the world in 1960, as the site of the Winter Olympics. It now ranks among the world's leading alpine ski resorts, with roughly 100 ski trails, 32 ski lifts, including a gondola and a tram, and hundreds of acres of skiable mountain terrain. During "Snowfest" (a local winter festival held in early March) and over Christmas-New Year, Squaw Valley hosts some spectacular torch-light parades in which veteran skiers holding lighted torches descend the slopes in formation, creating a scene to behold.

Squaw Valley is also home to the illustrious. World-class skiers Tamara McKinney and Melissa Dimino are intimately connected with the valley, having done much of their training on its slopes, and many of San Francisco's notables maintain vacation homes here. Writers Blair Fuller and Oakley Hall (author of *Warlock*) live here year-round, conducting a Writers' Workshop at the Squaw Valley Theater in the summer months, to which flock several distinguished writers, literary agents and publishers, as guest speakers.

Besides its ski areas, Squaw Valley also has, just to the northwest of it, the 40,000-acre, federally preserved Granite Chief Wilderness Area, with a dozen or so hiking trails meandering through it, some of them astonishingly scenic.

A mile south of Squaw Valley the highway crosses over onto the east side of the Truckee River and a little farther Alpine Meadows Road branches to the west, passing over a small bridge. At the turnoff here is the River Ranch Inn, with a notable restaurant where, during the summer, one can sit out on a large deck area facing south over the river and watch rafters slosh through the water at the end of their downriver ride, for this also serves as an egress point for many.

West of River Ranch lies the Alpine Meadows ski area, one of North Lake Tahoe's largest ski areas, second only to Squaw Valley. It has over 2000 acres of skiable terrain, and 100 different ski runs, including one that is two miles long. Alpine also enjoys an average snowfall of some 450 inches annually, and one of the longest ski seasons at the lake, remaining open well into spring, often until July 4. Much of the surrounding scenery, too, is breathtaking, with lush, timbered mountains and the alpine peaks, Ward (elevation 8637 feet) and Scott (elevation 8246 feet), rising to the back of the meadows. The ski area also operates a Handicapped Ski School here.

Tahoe City

Tahoe City is the oldest settlement of North Lake Tahoe, situated at the lake end of the Tahoe-Truckee Route. It was also the first of Lake Tahoe's communities to be christened "Tahoe" (the "city" was tacked on merely for grandeur in 1863 when the townsite was first surveyed and established). The town has a population of under 5,000, and only a dozen or so public streets, all told, ideally suited to exploring on foot. There is a charming little business district here, as well as some worthwhile historic buildings, all quite interesting to the visitor.

A place of special interest here, however, is the Fanny Bridge, located at the Tahoe City Y (intersection of Highways 89 and 28), especially attractive in summer. The bridge is built across the mouth of the Truckee River, the lake's only outlet, and across from it are the historic Outlet Gates, comprising a dam built in 1910 to regulate the water flow from the lake. The outlet was first dammed in 1870, with a rock and timber crib, by one Colonel Von Schmidt, a controversial figure who once proposed to channel the lake's waters to the San Francisco bay area via a tunnel through the Sierra. There is a clear-water pool directly beneath the bridge, saturated with schools of Rainbow Trout, quite enjoyable to children. Worth visiting, too, is the Gatekeeper's Cabin, located near the southern end of the Outlet Gates. Originally built in the early 1900's to house the gatekeeper (custodian of the waters, in charge of releasing the waters), the cabin burned to the ground in 1978 and was rebuilt a few years later to house the North Lake Tahoe Historical Society Museum. There are several old photographs and artifacts depicting Lake Tahoe's past on display at the museum, as well as a collection of Tahoe greeting cards, hand-drawn and painted by local artists. The museum is open May-September.

Also of historical interest is Watson's Log Cabin, located in the center of town, on the main street, North Lake Boulevard (Highway 28). The cabin was originally built in 1880 as the honeymoon cottage of Tahoe City pioneers, Robert and Stella Watson. It, too, is now a museum operated by the North Lake Tahoe Historical Society, with displays of local historical interest. Directly across from the cabin stands the Big Tree, plumb in the center of the street, a Tahoe City landmark for nearly 120 years and now also the community Christmas Tree. On the lake side of the cabin the Tahoe City bluff unfurls into a lovely, partly sandy, partly grassy area, known as the Tahoe City Commons. The recreation area was actually deeded to the people of Tahoe City several decades ago, hence the name "Commons." The Commons is also the site of the town's first wharf, built in 1864, and the scene of a famous gunfight (circa 1872) in which a local bartender shot and killed a notorious gunman, James Stewart, also known as the "Silent Terror." During the summer the beach area here is quite well liked, and on the Fourth of July all the townspeople gather here to watch the fireworks display.

Tahoe City also has some shopping malls of interest. The Cobblestone Mall, for instance, located on North Lake Boulevard, is a charming replica of a Bavarian Alpine Village, with stucco walls, dark walnut trim, a Tudor mural on its feature wall, and a clock-faced turret

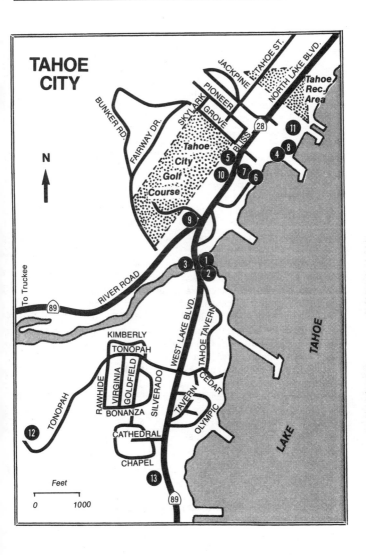

TAHOE CITY

N

Places of Interest -
1) Lake Tahoe Dam
2) Gatekeeper's Cabin
3) Fanny Bridge
4) Roundhouse Mall
5) Big Tree
6) Tahoe Commons Beach
7) Watson's Cabin
8) Tahoe City Boatworks
9) Tahoe City "Y"
10) Cobblestone Mall
11) Lighthouse Center
12) Granlibakken Lodge and Tennis Courts
13) Stone Chapel

above the north wing. Two others, the Boatworks Mall and the Roundhouse Mall, are farther to the east of Cobblestone, set slightly back from the highway. The Roundhouse Mall is actually housed in the old Southern Pacific Railroad building, dating from 1890, where a machine shop and a roundhouse were once to be found. There are some exquisite gift shops within and the Tahoe Boat Company Marina just at the front of the mall, where several antique wooden boats can be seen during the Concours d'Elegance, held in July each year. At the Boatworks Mall one can visit two or three fine art galleries, as well as some specialty shops. Adjoining the Boatworks to the northeast is the Lighthouse Center, also with some shopping possibilities, and farther east from the malls, more or less on the eastern boundary of Tahoe City, is the Tahoe State Park Recreation Area, a triangular grassy tract with some picnicking facilities.

Some of the other points of interest, just outside Tahoe City, include the site of the legendary Tahoe Tavern, an old, particularly charming stone chapel, and Lake Tahoe's oldest ski resort, Granlibakken, all located on West Lake Boulevard (Highway 89) just south of the Tahoe City Y. The Tahoe Tavern site has been built upon with the Tahoe Tavern Properties, a condominium development, on the east side of the highway. The Tavern is memorable mostly as the playground of the social sets from San Francisco and elsewhere during the 1920's and 1930's; it was then also considered to be one of the finest hotel-casinos at the lake. Built in 1901, the Tavern was razed in 1964. The Granlibak-ken Ski Resort is still in operation, however. It first opened to the public in 1926, boasting an "Olympic Hill" which comprised a ski jump and a toboggan run. Granlibakken (meaning "hillside sheltered by fir trees") is still the smallest ski area in the Tahoe basin, though it now has a worthwhile lodge, and tennis courts for summer use. South from Granlibakken, near Tahoe City's Episcopal Church, and also on the west side of the highway, is a small but lovely stone chapel with tiny recessed windows, some with stained-glass, dating from 1909. The chapel is now the property of the Church.

THE WEST SHORE

South from Tahoe City to the Rubicon Hills and the D.L. Bliss State Park, roughly 16 miles of shoreline and a dozen or so tiny, seasonally inhabited resort communities make up the west shore. This, then, is that wilderness country we have talked about, with lush, evergreen forests tumbling down the mountain sides to the very edge of the lake, with thickly wooded neighborhoods neatly tucked away into the bunched-up landscape, and with native black bears to be seen every once in a while in late fall, ambling along on the outskirts of one of the higher, more remote subdivisions; often while motoring in these parts, usually on August mornings, one can even spot a coyote or two dashing across the road. The highway through here, Highway 89, is narrow and twisty, looping around granite protrusions and following closely a jagged shoreline; south from the Tahoe City "Y" to the Sugar Pine Point State Park it becomes the West Lake Boulevard, whereupon it turns into Emerald Bay Road until the D.L. Bliss State Park, continuing on south from there to the south shore communities. Several enchanting side streets branch off into the timbered neighborhoods and the abounding wilderness, providing for some delightful, secluded vistas. To the back of here rise at least nine different mountain peaks, each some 2000 feet above lake level, and six or seven unpretentious creeks meander down to the lake, offering up good harvests of trout in spring. Besides which, there are two officially designated State Parks on the west shore, Sugar Pine Point and D.L. Bliss; a third, the Emerald Bay State Park, borders on the south side of the D.L. Bliss park. A great many well-wooded campgrounds and picnic areas are also to be found scattered throughout the area, with some lovely pebble beaches here and there.

The west shore is among the oldest of Lake Tahoe's vacation areas, where city folk came to sample the "wild" life of fishing and hunting as early as the 1870's. Thus, many of the area's earliest resorts, such as Sunnyside, Tahoe Pines, Homewood, Chamber's Landing, Sugar Pine Point and Meeks Bay, date back more than a century, with most of them still exhibiting a rural charm. And yet, creature comforts and modern resort facilities are just as readily available here. There are four full-fledged marinas on the west shore, catering to a wealth of water activity, and two alpine ski areas, Homewood and Granlibakken. Many miles of groomed cross-country ski trails can also be enjoyed through the area's State Parks and National Forest lands, with a number of them substituting for hiking trails in the summertime; and more than 10 miles of bike paths follow alongside of the highway for a more peaceful look at the lake. Additionally, for lodging and dining out, the west shore has some well-appointed lodges, and one or two European-style restaurants.

Sunnyside

Northernmost among the west shore's resorts is Sunnyside, a pleasant little area situated above Ward Creek, just one and one-half miles south of Tahoe City. It is named for the bay upon which it sits and upon which the original "Sunnyside" cottage, pier and boathouse were built in the late 1800's. Central to Sunnyside is the Sunnyside Resort (and Marina) which now fronts on the bay. The resort building, recently remodeled, dates from 1907, originally built as the summer home of Captain Kendrick, a wealthy sea captain; the resort now also has a worthwhile restaurant, with a delightful deck overlooking the lake. As for the marina snuggled up along the resort area—it first came to notice in 1925 when a group of affluent, amateur sailors from San Fransisco began congregating here, forming the prestigious Tahoe Yacht Club. It remains popular today with wealthy boat owners, who continue to moor their boats here.

The tract west of the Sunnyside Resort is known as Tahoe Park, with the Tahoe Park store fronting on the highway, close by the resort.

Across from the store is a cluster of box-like cabins, housing the North Tahoe Fine Arts Council, and the Fire Sign Cafe where hot mulled wine can be leisurely sipped by a roaring fire in winter. The cafe is popular with west shore visitors, open for breakfast and lunch.

South of Sunnyside lies the rectangle-shaped William Kent Campground, a favorite with summer vacationers, with a sandy beach spilling over onto the lake side of the highway. To the back of here is the rugged, beautiful Ward Canyon, arrived at by taking Wark Creek Boulevard, which is really a continuation of Pineland Drive, to the very end; the Twin Peaks (elevation 8878 ft.) are farther west from there. North of the canyon you can walk through the gently rolling Paige Meadows where native wildflowers are in bloom in spring and summer; the meadows double as a cross-country ski area in winter. Also of interest, a short distance to the south of the William Kent campground flows Ward Creek, upon which was built the west shore's first and only sawmill, Saxton's Mill, in 1864; the mill supplied railroad ties for the construction of Central Pacific's Sierra track in the mid-1860's.

South to Tahoe Pines

South of Sunnyside are three newer, well-wooded subdivisions, Pineland, Timberland and Skyland; and just below Skyland, the highway curves around a shallow crescent with a pebble beach and a picnic area, known as the Kaspian Recreation Area. Immediately west of there, the Blackwood Canyon cuts deep into the hinterland, with a lovely tree-lined road, by which to explore, passing through it. Almost directly ahead, perhaps a little to the north, the great Stanford Rock rises to a height of 8473 feet, and the Blackwood Creek meanders alongside, slowly filtering into the lake to the east. Quite like the Ward Canyon, Blackwood Canyon, too, has hiking possibilities in summer and cross-country skiing and snowmobiling in winter.

Just around the corner from the Kaspian Recreation Area, where the highway leaves the shoreline, a naked twist of rock rises above, on the west side of the road, some 250 feet high. This is the legendary Eagle Rock, named for "White Eagle," an extraordinarily large eagle that soared above the rock long, long ago, and then one day turned into an Indian brave. Legend holds that the chief of the Washoe Indian tribe that dwelled here in the early times had a beautiful daughter who would not choose, for marriage, from among the braves of the tribe. In her solitude she would climb to the top of the rock and gaze out into the distance, hoping to perhaps see a handsome Indian warrior approaching. It was about that time that the great "White Eagle" began frequenting the rock, squawking as it soared above. The tribespeople knew not where the eagle had come from, but they soon grew to like it, and even looked upon it as a good omen. Then one day, as the story goes, the eagle left the rock, only to return a few days later with an arrow through its wing, and in great pain. The tribespeople saw what had happened and were deeply concerned. The Indian princess, the chief's daughter, ascended the rock and went over to the wounded eagle. There was pain and sadness in the bird's eyes. The princess carefully removed the arrow then bent over and kissed the eagle gently on its head. And instantly, to her utter amazement, the eagle turned into a handsome young brave. The Indian brave told the princess about an evil medicine man who had cast a spell on him, turning him into an eagle, to be turned back into a brave only if kissed by an Indian princess. Thus the couple remained a while, fell in love, came down from the rock, married, and lived happily ever after. Of course, the rock was also used as a lookout by the Washoe to watch the movements of their adversaries, the Paiute, and until the very early 1900's, Washoe Indians cleaned and dried fish beneath the rock, caught mostly from the adjoining Blackwood Creek, using forks and baskets.

The lakefront tract across from the rock, much of it heavily forested and therefore hidden from view, is known as Idlewild. This is where many of the west shore's wealthiest families maintain summer homes. In the 1890's, Idlewild became a renowned mecca of high society. Here the wealthy and the fashionable from San Francisco gathered, led by one Aimee Crocker Gillig Gouraud Miskinoff, so obviously boasting a collection of husbands, who went on to write the book, *I'd Do It Again*, followed by *Paula Loves Pearls* which was inspired by her excursion to the South Seas where, it is told, she made the "great sacrifice" to a South Seas Island chieftain in exchange for a beautiful black pearl. Today, however, Idlewild is a much more quiet, almost sleepy neighborhood.

Adjoining Idlewild on the south is one of the west shore's grand estates, Fleur du Lac, its gray stone wall fronting on the highway. This, in fact, is the former Henry J. Kaiser estate, originally built in 1939 in a record time of 29 days. It then comprised six stone chalets, one for each of the top executives of Kaiser's six companies, built around an elaborate mansion which became the summer home of Mr. and Mrs. Kaiser. The estate, at the time, also featured such amenities as a drive-in boat storage, an amphibious plane landing and an inland waterway. Later, in the 1970's, the movie *Godfather II* was filmed on location at the estate. But much of what was, has been either demolished or "remodeled" since, and the property now has on it a cluster of multi-million-dollar condominiums. In any case, "Fleur du Lac" is not open to the public, although you can catch a glimpse or two of the estate's front structures and its rocked-in waterway and mini-lighthouse from the lake. In summer, a cruise aboard North Tahoe Cruises' *Sunrunner* is much to be recommended, for this includes a commentary on the estate's history and other interesting features, as it passes by the estate.

Opposite Fleur du Lac, on the west side of the highway, lies Tahoe Pines, established in 1911, and just to the south of there is the Tahoe Swiss Village, one of the west shore's most prestigious subdivisions.

Homewood

Homewood is a naturally sheltered resort settlement perched at the head of McKinney Bay, some two miles south of Tahoe Pines. It is unique in that its alpine ski area and marina, namely the Homewood Ski

Area and the High & Dry Marina, are separated by only some 20 feet of highway, the mere width of the road, (and if the mountain slopes were to have stretched another hundred yards or so farther, it is entirely possible that one could have taken a downhill as well as a water skiing lesson in one, single run). Homewood actually has two marinas and its ski area. The other marina, known simply as Obexer's and dating from the 1930's, is farther to the south, its faded-red boat storage buildings fronting on the highway. Among these buildings is one with dormers and a ragged exterior, originally built around 1920 as a "playhouse" for Walter Hobart, Jr., son of the flamboyant 19th century mining magnate and lumber baron, Walter Hobart, Sr.

Also of interest at Homewood is the Rockwood Lodge, located just to the north of the Obexer buildings, on the opposite side of the highway. It is quite picturesque with its rock-wall exterior—believed to be the work of the same stonemason who is credited with the building of the original Fleur du Lac structures farther north on the west shore—and lovely knotty pine interior. The lodge was originally built as a summer home in 1936, by one Carlos Rookwood, a prosperous dairyman (and sometime bootlegger) from Vallejo. The lodge is now a charming bed and breakfast establishment, beautifully restored to its former glory.

Also worth visiting at Homewood are a couple of countrified restaurants, including the Old Tahoe Cafe, a casual diner that has long been a favorite of skiers. Then, too, at the northern end of the Homewood Ski Area is a touch of old Switzerland, the Swiss Lakewood Restaurant, specializing in European cuisine. Opposite the Swiss restaurant is a unique seaplane base, the only one of its kind at the lake, from where seaplane rides can be taken over the lake for some spectacular aerial sightseeing; and during the summer months, noted opera singers and chamber orchestras from San Francisco and elsewhere perform in the outdoor area adjacent to the seaplane base, offering yet an added attraction to the west shore visitor.

Chambers Landing and Tahoma

Leaving Homewood, the highway circles a granite outcropping near the southeast corner of McKinney Bay, then turns directly south. About fifty yards or so from the curve, a side road leads off toward the lake, down to historic Chambers Landing, where one can visit a lovely sandy beach and a fabulous 1870's over-water clubhouse perched at the end of an odd-shaped pier, now serving as a cocktail bar and lounge. This is, of course, the oldest such clubhouse at the lake, a glorious reminder of the "Gay 90's" when scores of over-water saloons and clubhouses burst upon the Lake Tahoe shoreline. Expansive, all-round views can be enjoyed from here.

Just over a mile down the road from Chambers Landing lies Tahoma (meaning "home away from home"), a more or less self-contained settlement with a post office, a knotty pine store, a saloon and a pizzeria. Of interest here is the Alpenhaus, a traditional Swiss country inn and restaurant, housed in a beautifully-restored pre-World War II building which originally served as an ice house. The Alpenhaus also serves authentic Basque food on certain days of the week.

Sugar Pine Point State Park

The Sugar Pine Point State Park is one of the loveliest of Lake Tahoe's parks, bordered on the southwest by the northern portion of the high-country Desolation Wilderness, and on the north by the Tahoma tract. There are nearly 2000 acres of parkland here, abundant in splendid trees and wooded trails, with three or four points of historic interest as well. One of the highlights of the park, that no one should miss, is the Ehrman Mansion, a magnificent, gabled and turreted three-story edifice, built in 1903 and once acknowledged as "the finest High Sierra summer home in California." The mansion sits on a knoll just back from the lake, reached via a small side road, east off the highway. A lovely walk through an open meadow to the north of the mansion will also take you to it. The mansion faces east over the lake, with its front grounds tumbling down to the water's edge along a dramatic, green slope populated with groves of stately pines and gnarled cedars. Upon these grounds the Ehrmans and the Hellmans—two fabulously wealthy families from San Francisco, related by marriage, and owners of the estate —hosted lavish buffet luncheons in the summers during the "Roaring 20's". The grounds now provide for some beautiful, shaded picnic areas, to be enjoyed by the general public. At the bottom of the slope there is an old L-shaped pier and two equally ancient boathouses. Also along the shoreline here you can view the stump of a 4-foot wide juniper tree that was once described by the renowned naturalist John Muir as "the largest and the finest in the Sierra." Surrounding the mansion are a series of smaller structures worth investigating, including a water tower and a power generating plant, servants' quarters, stables and carriage house, and a caretaker's cabin; there is even a tennis court here. The mansion is now an interpretive center of sorts, open to the public during summer. It was acquired by the California State Parks Division in 1965, together with the rest of the estate, for a reported $8 million.

North and south of the mansion are two other places of interest: General Phipps' Cabin and the site of the old Bellevue Hotel. The hotel site is just south of the mansion, at the edge of the lake, now overgrown with tall pines and firs. The Bellevue Hotel, a lure of its day, was built on this site in 1888 and gutted by fire in 1893. Particularly well patronized was its white, over-water clubhouse with lattice verandahs; this was also the only building to have survived the fire, and was later shipped across to the southwest corner of the lake, plank by plank, and rebuilt as the Cascade House. The Phipps' cabin, north of the Ehrman Mansion, can still be visited, located near the lakeshore. The cabin was originally built in the early 1860's by General William Phipps, a famous

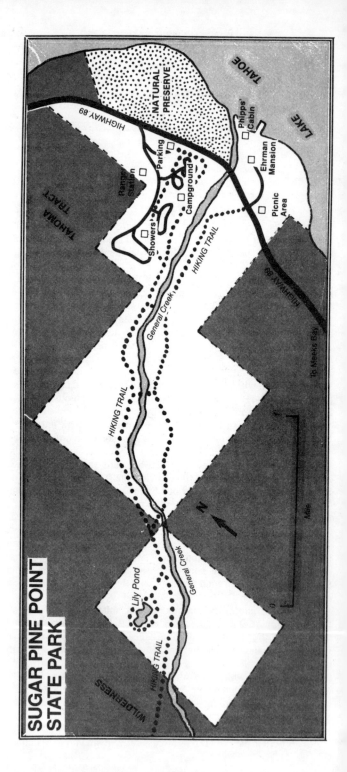

SUGAR PINE POINT STATE PARK

NATURAL PRESERVE

LAKE TAHOE

Phipps' Cabin

Ehrman Mansion

Picnic Area

HIGHWAY 89

Parking

Ranger Station

Showers

Campground

HIKING TRAIL

General Creek

HIKING TRAIL

HIGHWAY 89

To Meeks Bay

TAHOMA TRACT

HIKING TRAIL

N

Lily Pond

General Creek

HIKING TRAIL

WILDERNESS

Mile

0

Indian fighter from Kentucky, who settled here to lead a quiet life of fishing and hunting, homesteading some 160 acres along these shores. Named for the General are the General Creek Campground situated in the park on the west side of the highway, the Phipps' Lake which is farther out west in the Desolation Wilderness, the Phipps' Peak which lies just south of the Rubicon Peak, rising to a height of 9234 feet, and the General Creek that meanders enchantingly through here. There is also a Phipps' Pass in the high country wilderness.

The park, of course, is named for that most majestic of conifers, the Sugar Pine, known to grow to heights of around 200 feet and to live to a ripe old age of anywhere between 300 and 500 years. Its cones mature in approximately two years, often remaining on the tree for another year or so, unless broken off by birds or squirrels earlier. It is believed that in the early times the Washoe Indians liked to chew on the sweet sugar pine gum derived from these cones, as a sort of candy. Sugar Pines are said to have dominated the forest here until the 1880's, at which time large scale lumbering took its toll, stripping virtually all of Tahoe's forests of their virgin timber. Some fine second-growth Sugar Pines are now to be seen in the park, however, distinguished by their large, flat crowns and branches that join the trunks at right angles. Other growths in the park include Jefferey pines, lodgepoles, red and white firs, incense cedars, black cottonwoods, mountain alders and quaking aspen. In the open meadows, of which there are many in the park, one may find lupine, pussy paw, Indian paintbrush, and a variety of shrubs and wildflowers.

Sugar Pine Point has several enchanting walks to offer too (some of them substituting for nordic ski trails in winter), with stream crossings and wooded picnic areas to be encountered throughout. Notable among these trails is one that explores the "natural preserve" set aside on the east side of the highway. This is the Edward F. Dolder Nature Trail, especially interesting to nature buffs, for it passes through a sandy open meadow where many young, developing plant communities can be observed, which, some day, it is hoped, will evolve into lush forest growths. Another, the Beaudry Trail, passes to the south of the same meadow, with a dozen or so informative, historical markers to be seen alongside of it at intervals. Along this trail one can also view a weather-beaten section of a "Corduroy Road," built in 1882 as part of the great wagon road from Tahoe City to Sugar Pine Point; a "Corduroy Road" was built from logs laid adjacent to one another and held in place by tightly packed soil, usually in places where the earth was too loose to support a gravel road, such as here, where the granite sand has crept into the park. Beyond the "Corduroy" remnants the trail climbs a knoll atop which sits the Ehrman Mansion, and just east of here are a handful of small, sandy beaches. There are many other delightful walks to be enjoyed in the western section of the park as well, with one 5½-mile trail following alongside General Creek, presenting one with some idyllic scenery much of the way; a worthwhile diversion leads to the lovely Lily Pond. The park is also an ideal base from which to explore the northern parts of the more remote Desolation Wilderness, with trails leading to the Lost Lake, and Genevieve, Crag, Shadow, Hidden, Stony Ridge and Cliff lakes.

South to D.L. Bliss State Park

South from the Sugar Pine Point State Park one first arrives at Meeks Bay, a beautifully sheltered cove with a magnificent, mile-long white sand beach. This was the site of Washoe Indian summer camps in centuries past, with fishing and hunting being the principal pursuits. Several arrowheads from those times have been found on the beach here as recently as the early 1900's. Inland from the bay are flatlands covered with shrubs, once the scene of much farming, cattle grazing and dairying, and later on, in the 1870's and 1880's, the focus of vast logging operations. On the bay, too, is the historic Meeks Bay Resort, one of the most popular, flourishing campground resorts of Tahoe, with a store, a gift shop, bike rentals, a marina and beach, and some charming little cabins that date from the early 1900's. In fact, many of the structures at Meeks Bay date back to the earlier part of this century, including the Meadow Park Store and the cluster of tumbledown buildings nearby. There is a second campground at Meeks Bay, nestled along the promontory south of the crescent-shaped bay.

Immediately below Meeks Bay is the equally interesting but much wider Rubicon Bay. The south corner of the bay is described by a large, 600-foot promontory, beneath which the shoreline drops a sheer 1411 feet, vertically; this, incidentally, is the deepest point along the lake's shoreline, known as Rubicon Point. Above the bay can be seen a set of thinly forested hills, dotted with expensive mountain homes. These are the Rubicon Hills, and the lack of large-tree coverage here has really become quite an asset, with most of the homes enjoying unobstructed, panoramic views of the lake and the Sierra. Bearing the name "Rubicon" also, are a creek, a small wilderness lake, a mountain range, and the lakefront tract just below the highway here. And "Rubicon," we are told, is named for an ancient Roman river of the same name, made famous by Caesar's crossing of it. It is said that the back-country wilderness in these parts was so remote about a century or so ago, that the mountain men attempting to cross it, compared it to Caesar's perilous crossing of the river Rubicon, and so gave it the same name.

Adjoining Rubicon on the south is the D.L. Bliss State Park, a 957-acre preserve with 14,640 feet of shoreline. The park is named for one of Lake Tahoe's great legends, Duane LeRoy Bliss, a lumbering giant who at one time owned more than three-quarters of Tahoe's lakefront land. In fact, this very acreage was owned by the Bliss family until it was donated to the State of California in about 1930. It is of interest to note that Bliss also owned the largest fleet of Tahoe's steamers and tug boats, including the legendary *Tahoe*, as well as the narrow-gauge Lake Tahoe Railroad that shuffled down the Truckee River Canyon in the early 1900's, linking Tahoe City to the railroad town of Truckee. Even the famous Tahoe Tavern and Glenbrook estate were once owned by enormously wealthy Bliss family.

The Bliss State Park, however, is notable for mainly two things: its lovely, wooded campground, with nearly 200 campsites; and its unique rock formations. Of the latter it can be said that nowhere at the lake are so many large, well-rounded rocks to be found in one place, as here.

Particularly interesting among these is the Balancing Rock, an enormous mass of granite, wonderfully balanced on a natural pedestal, located just inside the park. The rock, especially striking in its size, vaguely resembles the head of a certain Indian chief who is said to have been buried here long, long ago. And here, again, is an enchanting Indian legend which tells of the formation of the rock. According to the legend, there once dwelled upon these shores a tribe of giant Indians, and in the waters off shore lived a wicked, giant serpent. Several tribesmen, while fishing in these waters, had been lost to the serpent's wrath over a period of time, and the tribe lived in great fear of the monster. One day, however, the great chief of the tribe who always sat in the very same spot where the rock is now to be seen, decided to slay the serpent and put an end to the misery of his people. He prepared his long knives and his bow and arrows, and went out in a boat to meet the serpent. He waited until the serpent showed its head above the water, then shot his arrows into its head. But the serpent remained alive. So then the chief lunged at the beast with a drawn knife, and a fierce battle ensued. The entire tribe gathered on the shore to watch their brave chief do battle with the wicked serpent. Many times the chief and the serpent disappeared beneath the water, but then resurfaced, until one final time they went down, not to appear again. Just then a storm broke out, lasting a whole day. When the storm subsided the following day, the bodies of both the chief and the serpent, bloodied and lifeless, washed up on shore. The tribespeople carried the body of their brave chief to his favorite spot where he had sat for so many years, looking out over the lake, and there they buried him, leaving his head above the ground so that he may continue to look out over his beloved "Big Blue." This, then, is the head of the giant chief, and the supporting pedestal his neck.

Also of interest at the Bliss State Park is a short, self-guided trail that leads to the site of an old lighthouse atop the Rubicon Point promontory. At the base of the outcropping is a walled-in area that offers picnicking possibilities and great views of the lake. This, by the way, is also the deepest point along Lake Tahoe's shoreline. The colors in the water here are remarkable, changing from a pale shade of blue to deep indigo, almost blue-black; (in 1889, a *Sacramento Daily Record Union* reporter is known to have joked about using these waters as a bluing solution for Yankee uniforms). Just north of here lie two delightful sandy beaches, and to the south a series of imaginatively named rocks, including Hen and Chickens, Four Loaves of Bread, Turk in Turban, Grinning Negro and Frog Rock. These are mostly visible from the lake. A little farther to the south is a shy little recess in the shoreline, known as "Grecian Bend"; it is named after the walk practiced by American women in the 1920's, and is said to resemble their padded rears. Also worth pursuing here is a beautiful 4½-mile walk that starts out by the beaches to the north, tracing the shoreline of the park south, then passes into the adjoining Emerald Bay State Park, leading eventually to Vikingsholm in the cradle of Emerald Bay. This is an especially picturesque walk, for it follows closely the lakeshore much of the way.

THE NORTH SHORE

The north shore, as the name suggests, describes the northern portion of the lake, from northeast of Tahoe City to Incline Village and Sand Harbor, encompassing nearly 20 miles of shoreline. Here the atmospheric clarity and the overtly generous high altitude sunshine become at once apparent, and are often cited as being the principal lures to the area. The north shore is also noted for its many natural wonders, among them the "Sunken Cliffs" off Dollar's Point, the "Hot Springs" of Brockway, the two-story high boulders off the north Stateline Point, the astonishing transparency of Agate and Crystal Bays, and the dozens of secluded coves just south of Sand Harbor where clusters of rocks emerge above the water to naturally enclose swimming areas. Then, too, there are the man-made wonders: three alpine ski areas—Northstar, Mount Rose and Diamond Peak at Ski Incline—four superb golf courses, a couple of miniature golfing alleys, several picnic and recreation areas, including the fabled Ponderosa Ranch (the set for TV's *Bonanza* series), and even some casinos.

A half dozen or so small detours provide for additional interest in the north shore. The area's main artery, Highway 28, part of which forms the North Lake Boulevard and part of it the Tahoe Boulevard, actually has two other highways branching from it—267 (North Shore Boulevard) and 27 (Mount Rose Highway). 267 passes over the 7199-foot Brockway Summit and so to Truckee, with Northstar-at-Tahoe lying at an approximate halfway point. The Mount Rose Highway winds through several miles of pine country to escape over the eastern Sierra range and into Nevada's desert valleys; the low-lying, barren hills farther east from the valleys lie in deep contrast to the High Sierra. Other detours lead to Marlette Lake, the Spooner Lake State Park, and along Incline's shoreline by way of the famous "Lakeshore Drive," each inviting special attention.

The Northwest

Leaving Tahoe City on North Lake Boulevard (Highway 28), the first subdivision encountered is Lake Forest, a wooded tract set slightly back from the highway. Lake Forest is an old settlement, dating back to 1859 when a real floating island, Island Farm, operated as a guest ranch just off the shores from here. The area was then also famous for giant vegetables grown on its soil, among which was one memorable, record-sized turnip measuring 16½ inches in diameter. Foremost among Lake Forest's attractions today is the Fish and Game Department's Hatchery, located at the corner of the highway and Lake Forest Road, and housed in a turn-of-the-century gnarled cedar building; it can be toured by prior arrangement with the department. South from the hatchery, down to the lake, extends the open meadow of the Lake Forest Campground, a favorite with summer vacationers. There is a small beach near the campground, and close at hand, too, are the U.S. Coast Guard Station and a public boat-launching ramp.

A quarter mile above Lake Forest is Dollar Hill, named for Robert Stanley Dollar, Sr., a San Francisco shipping magnate who owned much of this tract from 1927 until its subdivision only a few decades ago. Dollar Hill actually drops off sharply to the northeast and southwest along the highway, and to the southeast along a peninsular tract that converges into a point, variously known as Chinquapin, Old Lousy, Observatory and Dollar's Point. Here, it is told, that one George Flick proposed to build an observatory at a cost of $1,000,000 in 1873, but ended up placing it on Mount Hamilton above Santa Clara. Off Dollar's Point, however, are to be found some of the most treasured underwater marvels of Lake Tahoe, often clearly visible on fine, calm days. A slow boat ride along here, from just south of the Point to just past it, reveals what have come to be known as the "Sunken Cliffs." The lake floor drops from a depth of around 30 feet to a sheer 600 feet within some 50 yards or so, creating illusions of falling off a cliff; this, in fact, is what Mark Twain was referring to in his *Roughing It*, when he wrote about his fantastic "balloon voyages" on the lake. Two such "cliffs" run almost parallel to one another, like miniature canyons, some one-half mile apart. Beyond the "cliffs" can be discerned broad steps descending into the deep blue, known as the "Tahoe Flats"—an excellent area for trolling for Mackinaw trout in spring and early summer.

North of Dollar Point the highway curves around a twin cove to a protruding land mass known as Flick Point, which takes its name from the Flick Brothers who fished here, commercially, for several years. Interestingly, the Flick Brothers, William, John and Nicholas, were each born on Christmas Day in 1841, 1847 and 1850, respectively, with William passing away in April of 1929, John on April 9, 1938, and Nicholas on April 19, 1938; a coincidence worthy of record books. The bay here is Carnelian Bay, named for the reddish-brown semi-precious stones found in abundance on its sandy beach by a survey party in 1860. Carnelian Bay, of course, is also the scene of one of the most endearing tales of Lake Tahoe: "the hole in the bottom of the lake." It was about a mile off the Carnelian shores, as the tale goes, that a whirlpool was discovered in 1869 by one William Meeker, a vacationing stock speculator from San Francisco. Meeker quickly learned that the whirlpool had its origins in a hole in the bottom of the lake, one that tunneled beneath the lake floor to emerge in a Virginia City silver mine, the Savage Mine, many miles to the east. This startling discovery Meeker shared with one Colonel Clair, an unscrupulous stock trader, also from San Francisco. And the colonel had an idea... The two men carved out a conical-shaped "plug" from a 5-foot log to plug the hole with. Armed with this they were able to flood the shaft of the Savage Mine, or dry it out, practically at will, and thereby manipulate the company's stock: when the plug was out of the hole, the mine would remain flooded, the stock would plummet and the colonel and Meeker would buy; when the plug was in the hole, the mine would dry out, the stock would sky-rocket and they would sell out. Thus, within a week the colonel and Meeker cleaned up a cool couple of million dollars through manipulation of the Savage Mining Company's stock. Then one night the colonel cleaned out Meeker, knocked him unconscious, lowered his body into the hole in the bottom of the lake, and plugged the hole with the hand-crafted stopper. The body, of course, washed up in the sump of the Savage Mine several days later, mysteriously, needless to say; but the plug has remained in place ever since, its location a well-guarded secret of Colonel Clair's. Curiously, there is a Colonel Clair's restaurant located on the highway just north of Carnelian Bay, housed in a stately cedar building with a green shingled roof.

Inland from Carnelian Bay, high on a rise of ground, sits the Agate Bay subdivision where in the 1920's the Agate Bay Hotel was located, said to have been patronized by such luminaries as Theodore Roosevelt and Jack Dempsey. The hotel burned down in the 1940's.

A mile farther, just north of Flick Point, lies Tahoe Vista, with motels on both sides of the highway, many of them built some three decades ago for the Squaw Valley Winter Olympic Games of 1960. There are also some excellent gourmet restaurants here, notable among them Le Petit Pier, Captain Jon's and La Playa, the last of these housed in the old, native stone Kellogg Mansion, once the summer home of the legendary cereal king, built around 1910. There are, in addition, two marinas at Tahoe Vista, the Tahoe Vista Marina and Alpine Marina. The Tahoe Vista Marina is especially interesting with its long, L-shaped pier, which was built in the early 1900's to enable the 169-foot steamer *Tahoe* to dock in these waters while making its scheduled "mail stops." Propped at the marina, of course, is Captain Jon's, and beside it Le Petit Pier, both overlooking the lake. A couple of fine sandy beaches grace the Tahoe Vista shoreline, popular with summer crowds, and receded back from the shoreline is the North Tahoe Regional Park, with the well-liked Old Brockway Golf Course just to the east of there.

Northstar-at-Tahoe

6 miles north of the Tahoe Vista-Kings Beach area, just off Highway 267, lies Northstar-at-Tahoe, a 2500-acre, self-contained resort complex with clusters of condominiums, on-site lodging for tourists, alpine and nordic ski areas, a couple of restaurants, a general store, horse stables, and even an 18-hole golf course. Northstar is one of the north shore's newest resorts, built mostly in the early 1970's. It is also one of the world's first computer-designed recreation areas where such considerations as drainage, erosion, foliage, snowfall accumulations and grades were computer-analyzed to determine the best locations for the ski slopes, the condominium developments, paved streets, golf course and other recreational facilities. Through much of the 1970's the federal Environmental Protection Agency used Northstar as a demonstration project to illustrate the conservation of environment in modern development, and in 1971 the highly respected Sierra Club described it as a "model development."

Northstar has also been described as an "intermediate skier's paradise," and is one of Lake Tahoe's largest ski areas. Of interest, too, is Northstar's Recreation Center, comprising an Olympic swimming

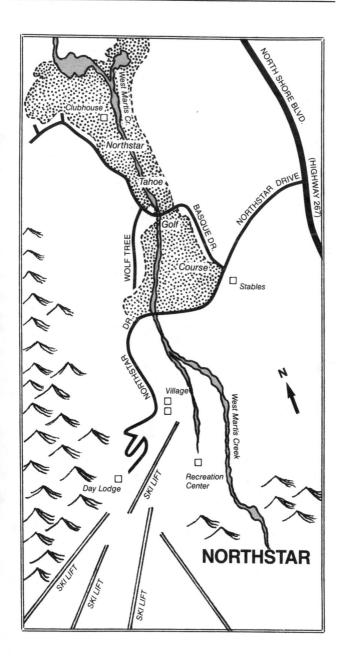

NORTHSTAR

pool, a 25-foot jacuzzi and a dozen or so tennis courts. During summer an arts and crafts market flourishes at the Northstar village, and in spring, hiking and horseback trails can be enjoyed through the abounding fir-clad mountain country and broad meadows covered with snowplant stalks and freshly-blossomed native wildflowers. To be also recommended at Northstar is the Schaffer's Mill restaurant, a distinguished steakhouse and seafood establishment where live music is featured on many evenings; the restaurant takes its name, quite appropriately, from Schaffer's Camp, a logging camp that flourished in these parts in the 1870's, supplying lumber for the Virginia City mines.

Kings Beach, Brockway and Crystal Bay

Back on Highway 28 (North Lake Boulevard), we enter the Kings Beach area to the west of the intersection of Highways 28 and 267. Kings Beach is one of the liveliest sections of North Lake Tahoe, where much haphazard development has occurred in previous years. The highway here widens into four lanes, with a profusion of shops, restaurants, fast-food places and motels on either side of the highway. One of the chief attractions at Kings Beach, of course, is its beach area, known as the Kings Beach State Recreation Area, where you can enjoy one of the longest and most beautiful sandy beaches on the north shore. In the summer months the beach is inundated with sun-seekers, windsurfers, joggers, walkers, bikini-clad girls, and scores of vacationers sprawled beneath brightly-colored beach umbrellas.

Indeed, Kings Beach, increasingly, is a summer community. Many of the stores here spill over onto the sidewalks in summer, displaying a myriad of Tahoe souvenirs and sporting goods, and eateries, too, move out of doors, sporting striped canopies and freshly-painted patio chairs and tables. In the open space adjacent to the intersection of Highways 28 and 267 the Pro Arts Festival is held in July and August each year, featuring several canvas-covered stalls where local artists and craftsmen display a bounty of hand-crafted merchandise, including pottery, leather goods, stained glass, semi-precious jewelry, wood carvings, imitation Navajo rugs, torch-molded copper decorations, some admirable sculpture, and even oil paintings and water colors inspired by the surrounding scenery. There are also a couple of art galleries of interest here, and one or two excellent restaurants.

At the eastern end of Kings Beach is the Brockway Hill, rising sharply to the north Stateline where gambling casinos border on the Nevada side. Brockway is really the western tract of the Stateline, dropping away southward to the Stateline Point. And here on the south side of the highway, west of the large promontory jutting out at the Stateline, are the famous Brockway Hot Springs, endowed with medicinal qualities and bubbling forth at a sizzling 147°F. From the late 1800's to the mid-1900's the Brockway Hot Springs Hotel stood at the site of the springs, luring health-seekers and vacationers alike, and prompting the building of the Hot Springs-Martis Valley Road (Highway 267) earlier in 1869. But in 1970 the hotel gave way to the present day luxury

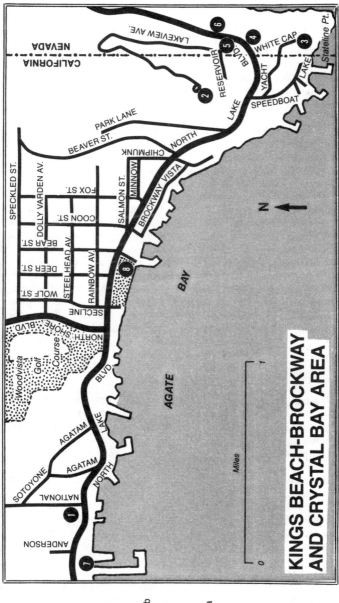

KINGS BEACH-BROCKWAY AND CRYSTAL BAY AREA

Points of Interest
1) Library
2) Stateline Fire Lookout
3) Cal-Neva Club
4) Crystal Bay Club
5) Tahoe Biltmore
6) Kelly's Nugget
7) Tahoe Vista Marina
8) Kings Beach Recreation Area

condominium development, the Brockway Springs Resort, where the hot mineral water is piped into every apartment, available at the turn of a faucet. Vacation rentals are available at the resort, however.

Brockway is also noted for its shoreline (the Brockway-Stateline shoreline), where several fascinating rock formations can be observed; these date back thousands of years to the ice age, when a gigantic glacier filled the lake's trough, pushing huge masses of rocks and boulders ahead of it as it moved northeast. Some of the submerged boulders, easily visible through the crystal clear waters, are extraordinary in size—as large as two-story houses.

The Nevada side of the Stateline is known as Crystal Bay, named for the bay onto which it fronts. Here at Crystal Bay are four small casinos—the Cal-Neva, the Crystal Bay Club, Tahoe Biltmore and Jim Kelly's Nugget. Although not quite of the stature of South Lake Tahoe's fastidious, multi-storied hotel-casinos, these north shore clubs nevertheless provide a wide range of gambling opportunities and even some live entertainment. The Cal-Neva, the largest of the north shore clubs, actually straddles the stateline just to the south, nearer Stateline Point; the stateline, in fact, runs through the club and can be seen painted on the rock wall in its lobby.

Northwest of the Crystal Bay casinos, a little way from the highway, is the Stateline Fire Lookout, a rare vantage point for those superb, sweeping views of Lake Tahoe. Reservoir Lane which flanks the Tahoe Biltmore parking lot on the east, Lakeview Avenue, and a Forest Service road that branches off Lakeview and loops back into the California side of the Stateline, lead to the Lookout.

Incline Village

Incline Village lies at the head of Crystal Bay (the actual bay), some two miles from the stateline. It is, of course, one of the most affluent of the north shore communities, where residents own their ski area, Ski Incline, as well as two golf courses and a couple of beaches. The sense of well being, however, is perhaps never more apparent than on Lakeshore Drive, where palatial homes stand in unabashed oppulence on the lake side of the road. On Lakeshore Drive, too, at the corner of Country Club Drive, is the Hyatt-Tahoe Hotel-Casino.

Incline Village, interestingly, derives its name from the "Incline Mountain" located just northeast of the business district, upon which an early day engineering marvel manifested itself. Here on Incline Mountain was built a tramway in 1874, straight up the side of the mountain, some 4000 feet in length, with a vertical rise of 1400 feet and a gradient of approximately 67%. Two tracks ran parallel to one another to the summit, and angled flat cars, specially designed for the task, carried full loads of logs to the very top, discharging them into a V-shaped log-chute which in turn passed through a 4000-foot water tunnel down the other side of the mountain, from where the logs were then railroaded across to the Virginia City mines. Two giant bullwheels were used in the operation, each 12 feet in diameter, with wire cables fed around them and hitched to the tops of the cars (a total of more than

8000 feet of cable was used). The summit wheel was driven by a 40-horsepower steam engine anchored in granite blocks, and the upward haul of each laden car was aided greatly by the counterweight of the downward bound car—a principle commonly employed in cable car operations. This, then, was "The Great Incline Tramway," an early day sight, pointed out by cruise-boat captains to their vacationing passengers as they rounded Crystal Bay. The tramway was dismantled in 1897 after nearly 200,000,000 board feet of lumber and more than a million cords of wood had been transported by way of it.

The lure of Incline Village today is its vacation ambiance, with facilities to complement. There are two alpine ski areas here, Mount Rose and Diamond Peak at Ski Incline, and two superb golf courses, the 18-hole, 7120-yard Incline Championship Course, and the smaller Incline Executive Course. Besides which, Incline also has tennis and racquetball facilities, as well as good shopping possibilities.

Incline also enjoys a relatively large spread, nearly nine square miles in area, with some leisurely drives to be taken through it, quite at random really. The tree-lined Country Club Drive, for one, enchantingly passes by both golf courses, the soft green pastels making for some delightful viewing; Fairway Boulevard, Driver Way and Golfers Pass Road actually cut through the manicured greens for a more intimate drive yet. Ski Way is another worthwhile drive, with many miles of mountain country to be enjoyed enroute to the ski slopes; along here, too, is the Potlatch, an exotic gallery-store featuring Southwest art and jewelry, and the Tyrolian Village where cheerful, European-style chalets stand in a cluster. Farther out from the village the Mount Rose Highway climbs to more than 1000 feet above lake level, winding through lush, pine-clad terrain, then descends into the sculpted, barren valleys east of the Sierra, providing the motorist with a bewildering contrast that brings out the mystique in mountain country. Along the Mount Rose Highway there is also a vista point, with fabulous, panoramic views of Lake Tahoe.

Ponderosa Ranch

Another attraction at Incline Village, nestled along its southeast corner and much to be recommended for family entertainment, is the Ponderosa Ranch, a lovely western theme park with an Old West town, western museums, food concessions, stables and acres upon acres of ranchland rolling back into the mountains to the east. The ranch, of course, was the setting for many years for the TV series, *Bonanza*, starring Lorne Green and Michael Landon. In fact, much of what you see here was built expressly for the series by NBC in 1959. Just above town, at the southern end, you can visit the Cartwright family's rambling log home, where numerous indoor scenes were filmed on location. The house itself has in it some superb period furniture, including a fine hand-crafted dining table, and a carved coat-rack upon which hang the vests and hats of the Cartwrights from the series. The house also features a splendidly large stone fireplace in its living room.

Below the Cartwright House lies the Old West town, with board-

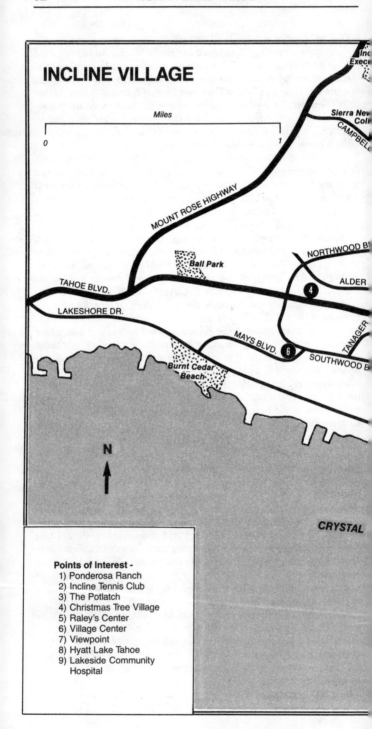

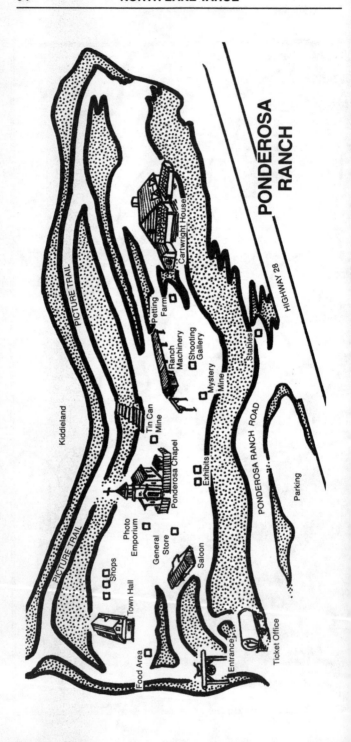

walks, a couple of 1860's saloons, a sheriff's office, a barber's shop, a taxidermist shop, an assay office, a "tin can" mine with a weathered, wooden tailing wheel, and a charming, 19th century chapel which can usually be booked for weddings. There is also a games arcade in the old town, featuring a shooting gallery, and an old-fashioned ice-cream parlor as well as a souvenir store. A few museums here have lavish displays of ancient firearms and carriages and coaches of sorts, mostly from the "wild west" days, while the town's gravel road is strewn with an assortment of early-day ranch equipment, century-old firepumpers, covered wagons, U.S. Cavalry wagons, and literally a wealth of other antique objects. One of the highlights of the tour through the town is the Mystery Mine, or "anti-gravity house," where a mine shaft has been constructed such, with angled floor-boards, ceiling and walls, so as to create a sense of imbalance, even dizziness; here one must stand at an approximate 45-degree angle to the floor to attain balance, for it is virtually impossible to stand dead straight without falling over.

The ranch also has an outdoor food area at the northern end of the old town, where juicy "Hossburgers" can be enjoyed. Additionally, Ponderosa Ranch offers guided horseback trail rides through its delightful back-country, which are all the more rewarding as they offer some spectacular views of the lake and the Sierra from several points enroute.

Sand Harbor and South

Two and one-half miles south of the Ponderosa Ranch lies Sand Harbor, North Lake Tahoe's favorite summer recreation area, where several open-air music festivals and theater performances are held each year in July and August; *Romeo and Juliet, As You Like It, Taming of the Shrew*, and other Shakespeare plays are enacted by members of well-known theater groups from San Francisco and elsewhere. In the late 1800's, Sand Harbor was the scene of dozens of lavish parties hosted by Walter Hobart, Sr., a mining magnate who made his first million in the Comstock at the age of 21; Hobart was also associated with Tahoe's lumbering activity, and he even owned the famous Incline Tramway.

Sand Harbor has some lovely picnic areas and a couple of sweeping sandy crescents to enjoy, with tiny piles of rocks to be seen near the mouths of the crescents, enclosing quiet little pools of water in which to splash around. North and south of the beach areas are nestled a handful of rock-lined, sheltered coves, among them Hidden Beach, lying about a mile to the north of the harbor and reached via a foot trail from the highway; on-shore fishing is excellent along these rocky banks. Also, from Sand Harbor three or four delightful hiking trails wander off into Lake Tahoe State Park, which lies just to the east. One of these trails leads to two small but enchanting lakes, the Twin Lakes, passing by some idyllic scenery; another follows along Tunnel Creek in the northeast to arrive at the site of the long-forgotten Tunnel Creek Station, where you can view the ruins of old log-flumes dating from the 1880's.

South along Highway 28 are several more secluded coves and shaded areas, some with small beaches which are mostly frequented by nudists; best known among these is Chimney Bay, nearly three miles south of Sand Harbor. Also along the shoreline (almost directly opposite the Marlette Reservoir), hidden from view and closed to the public, is the legendary "Thunderbird Lodge," now known as Whittel's Castle. It was built in 1939, at an estimated cost of $300,000, by Captain George Whittel, a multi-millionaire from San Francisco. Whittel, at one time, is believed to have owned as much as 14,623 acres of land here, of which at least 452 acres bordered on the lake, taking in 11 miles of shoreline. Of course, much of this land is now either state-owned or under the jurisdiction of the National Forest Service, making this one of the longest, uninterrupted green belts at the lake.

Southeast from Whittel's Castle and the Marlette Reservoir, and receded back a mile or so from the highway, lies Marlette Lake, one of the highest lakes in the region, at an elevation of 7700 feet. Marlette Lake in the early days was the lifeblood of the Virginia City mines, supplying the entire mining town with its water needs; in 1887, a record 6,600,000 gallons of water was drained from the lake daily. A rather scenic hiking trail now journeys along the west shore of Marlette Lake.

Also worth visiting here is the Spooner Lake State Park, which, too, is arrived at by way of a detour from Highway 28, eastward. South from Spooner Lake, a great deal of momentuous scenery presents itself, especially astounding where, after the highway leaves the Spooner Junction (intersection of Highways 28 and 50), the lake bursts into view again.

DETOURS

Reno

Reno, situated some 35 miles northeast of Lake Tahoe and reached by way of Interstate 80 east or the Mount Rose Highway (Route 431), is one of the best nearby attractions for visitors to the area. Reno has a population of roughly 150,000, and claims for itself the title, "The Biggest Little City in the World." The city, of course, is filled with casinos, hotels and restaurants—some 20,000 hotel rooms and over 300 restaurants—with live entertainment to be found at several of these. Of particular interest here is Bally's Hotel and Casino, where some fabulous shows can be enjoyed, including "Hello Hollywood Hello," in which a real live DC-9 appears on the stage; Bally's also boasts one of the largest casinos in the world, the size of two football fields. Worth visiting, too, is Harrah's Automobile Collection on Mill and Lake Streets, where, in a 100,000-square-foot facility, more than two hundred antique cars, some of them truly classics, are on display—everything from Bugattis to Model A's to Deusenbergs, Pierce Arrows and Franklins; among these is John Wayne's Cadillac convertible, and the 1929 Deusenberg Dual Cowl Phaeton and 1930 DuPont Royal Town Car, both of which were featured as Daddy Warbucks' personal vehicles in the movie "Annie." Another point of interest is the Harrold's Gun

M.S. Dixie on the lake

Winter at Squaw Valley, site of the 1960 Winter Olympic Games

Scenic Lake Tahoe, viewed from Mt. Pluto on the north shore

Skiing at Northstar-at-Tahoe

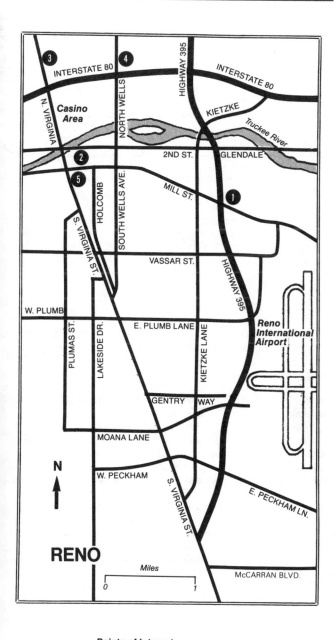

Points of Interest –
1) Bally's Grand Hotel
2) Harrah's Automobile Collection
3) University of Nevada
4) Washoe County Fairgrounds
5) Pioneer Theatre Auditorium

Collection, located in Harrold's Club on North Virginia Street, which features several antique guns, including Wild Bill Hickcock's .32 Smith and Wesson and a .45 Colt that once belonged to the legendary Jesse James. Take the time also to visit the Pioneer Theatre Auditorium, situated on Virginia Street just south of the casinos, quite distinctive with its gold geodesic dome; it was built in 1967 at an estimated cost of $2.5 million, and can accommodate up to 1,400 people. Another place of interest is Reno's University, dating from 1864. The university is located just to the north of town, on North Virginia Street.

Reno also hosts several excellent spectator events much of the year. One or two worthy of mention are the Reno National Championship Air Races and Air Show, claimed to be the world's most daring and thrilling motorsports races, and the Reno Rodeo, one of the most colorful in the country. The air races are held in late September, and the rodeo in June. In September, too, during the second weekend, is the Great Reno Balloon Race, a memorable visual experience, featuring more than a hundred multi-colored hot-air balloons. For more information on Reno events, contact the Reno-Tahoe Visitors Center at (702) 348-7788.

Virginia City.

Another place of interest, quite close to Lake Tahoe, is Virginia City, much to be recommended to first-time visitors to the area. It is roughly 30 miles to the east of Lake Tahoe's Incline Village, reached by taking the Mount Rose Highway (Route 431) to the intersection of Highway 395, then Route 341 over the Geiger Grade to Virginia City. Virginia City, billed as "the liveliest ghost town in the world," was once a bustling, thriving metropolis of 30,000, and the largest city between San Francisco and St. Louis, Missouri. It now has a population of only 900. Yet, nearly 500,000 tourists visit the town every year. Tours of ancient silver mines, rides on the Virginia & Truckee Railroad steam trains, and visits to the many splendid Victorian mansions, notable among which are the Savage and Mackay mansions, are all worthwhile tourist activities. The downtown has several 1860's saloons and antique shops of sorts, as well as covered wooden walkways, reminiscent of the Old West. There is a huge cemetary worth seeing here too, and dozens of other old buildings and museums, with countless antique exhibits. In September, the annual Camel Races provide for some fun and games, with side attractions such as parachuting and mock battles between the Confederates and Yankees. The town also has an historic newspaper, the "Territorial Enterprise," on which Mark Twain worked briefly in the 1860's. The Virginia City Visitors Bureau, located on C Street, has films on Virginia City's bonanza days, which are shown at the center daily.

PRACTICAL INFORMATION FOR NORTH LAKE TAHOE

HOW TO GET THERE

Tahoe City, Kings Beach and Incline Village lie approximately 200 miles northeast of San Francisco, or 120 miles or so from Sacramento. The best and most direct way to reach the North Lake Tahoe area is by way of *Interstate 80*, which leads directly to the town of Truckee, then *Highway 89* south some 14 miles to Tahoe City, or *Highway 267* to Kings Beach, roughly 13 miles, then *Highway 28* another 7 miles from Kings Beach to Incline Village.

Both *Greyhound* and *Amtrak* have scheduled daily services to Truckee from San Francisco, Sacramento, and other major cities. For a timetable, call Greyhound locally at (916) 587-3822; for Amtrak schedules, call (800) 252-2231 in California, or (800) 648-3850 from out of the state.

The nearest commercial airport to North Lake Tahoe, the Reno International Airport, lies approximately 50 miles to the northeast. Several different commercial airlines service this airport, including *American* (800) 433-7300, *America West* (702) 348-2777, *Continental* (800) 525-0280, *Delta* (800) 221-1212, *Eastern* (800) 323-7323; *Northwest* (800) 225-2525; *Sky West* (800) 453-9417, *United* (800) 241-6522, and *US Air* (800) 428-4322. Shuttle-bus services between the Reno airport and North Lake Tahoe are offered by *Reno Tahoe Tour Company* (800) 821-1555/(702) 322-2828, and *See Tahoe Tours* (702) 832-0713.

TOURIST INFORMATION

Greater North Lake Tahoe Chamber of Commerce, Lighthouse Center, Tahoe City; (916) 583-2371. Tourist information brochures, including listings of accommodations and restaurants; maps, calendar of events. *North Tahoe Visitors & Convention Bureau,* P.O. Box 5578-57, Tahoe City, CA 95730; (800) 822-5959 from California/(800) 824-8557 from outside California. Tourist information, ski packages. The Bureau also offers an accommodations reservation service; call the toll-free numbers.

Incline Village Chamber of Commerce, at 999 Tahoe Boulevard in Incline Village (702) 831-4440. Brochures, calendar of events, general tourist information.

Truckee-Donner Chamber of Commerce, Commercial Row, Truckee (916) 587-2757. Tourist literature, including schedule of local events, and listings for area accommodations and restaurants.

Reno-Tahoe Visitors Center, 135 N. Sierra, Reno (702) 348-7788. Tourist information and brochures, calendar of events and listings of area accommodations and restaurants. *Reno-Sparks Chamber of Commerce*, 133 N. Sierra, Reno (702) 329-3558/(702) 786-3030. *Virginia City Visitors Bureau*, South C St., Virginia City (702) 847-0177.

Road Conditions. For information on winter driving conditions in the area, and chain controls and road closures, call (916) 581-1400.

ACCOMMODATIONS

Truckee

Super 8 Lodge. *$49-$69*. Deerfield Drive, West Truckee; (916) 587-8888/(800) 843-1991. 41 rooms, TV, phones, sauna, spa.

Best Western Truckee Tahoe Inn. *$58-$66*. 11331 Hwy. 267 (1 mile south of Truckee); (916) 587-4525/(800) 528-1234. 100 rooms; phones, sauna, jacuzzi. Continental breakfast.

Truckee Hotel. *$52-$89*. Cnr. Commercial Row and Bridge St., Truckee; (916) 587-4444. Refurbished Victorian hotel, built in 1872. Some rooms with private baths. Continental breakfast. Restaurant.

Tahoe City and West Shore

Alpenhaus. *$60-$120*. 6941 West Lake Blvd., Tahoma; (916) 525-5000. Traditional Swiss country inn, housed in a restored pre-World War II building. 7 rooms and 2 suites in main building, and 5 self-contained cottages. Restaurant on premises.

Blue House Inn. *$80-$225*. 7660 River Road (Hwy. 89), Tahoe City; (916) 582-8415. Charming bed and breakfast inn overlooking the Truckee River, near Squaw Valley. 5 individually-decorated guest rooms in main house, and a self-contained unit, with a canopied four-poster bed, private bath and kitchen, located over the carriagehouse. Full breakfast.

Cottage Inn. *$75-$115*. 1690 West Lake Blvd., Tahoe City; (916) 581-4073. Bed and breakfast inn with 8 duplex units and 6 individual rooms. Full breakfast, served in the dining room or in bed. Also sauna. Close to beach.

Edwards Tahoe Lodge. *$55-$85*. 6845 West Lake Blvd., Tahoma; (916) 525-7207. 17 cottages with kitchens and fireplaces. Pool.

Homeside Motel & Lodge. *$50-$60*. West Lake Blvd., Homewood; (916) 525-9990. 17 rooms, TV, sauna.

Lake of the Sky Motor Inn. *$58-$68*. 955 North Lake Blvd., Tahoe City; (916) 583-3305. 22 rooms, TV, phones, pool.

Mayfield House. *$75-$95*. 236 Grove Street, Tahoe City; (916) 583-1001. Established Old Tahoe bed and breakfast inn, housed in historic stone cottage. 6 rooms, some private baths. Full breakfast, with homemade pastries. Centrally located.

Pepper Tree Inn. *$57-$65*. 645 North Lake Blvd., Tahoe City; (916) 583-3711. 51 rooms, several with lakeviews; TV, phones, pool, and sun deck.

River Ranch. *$80-$90*. Alpine Meadows Road and Highway 89; (916) 583-4264. Refurbished Old Tahoe lodge on the banks of the Truckee River. 22 rooms, with TV and phones; restaurant and patio, overlooking river.

Rockwood Lodge. *$100-$150*. 5295 West Lake Blvd., Homewood; (916) 525-5273. Delightful, 50-year-old stone lodge, with 5 guest rooms. Antique decorated; feather beds, down comforters, Laura Ashley fabrics. Breakfast includes homemade croissants and freshly squeezed fruit juices. No smoking.

Sunnyside Lodge. *$75-$155*. 1850 West Lake Blvd., Sunnyside (2 miles south of Tahoe City); (916) 583-7200/(800) 822-2754 in CA. Luxury resort in lakeside setting; completely remodeled. 23 rooms, individually decorated; private balconies overlooking lake. Excellent restaurant on premises, serving breakfast, lunch and dinner.

Tahoe City Inn. *$58-$120*. 790 North Lake Blvd., Tahoe City; (916) 583-8578. 33 rooms; in-room spas, waterbeds. Some lake views.

Tahoe City Travelodge. *$65-$79*. 455 North Lake Blvd., Tahoe City; (916) 583-3766. 47 rooms, TV, phones, pool and hot tub.

Tamarack Lodge Motel. *$34-$44*. 2311 North Lake Blvd., Tahoe City; (916) 583-3350. 19 rooms, some with kitchenettes; TV.

North Shore

Blue Vue Lodge. *$42-$95*. 8755 North Lake Blvd., Kings Beach; (916) 546-3871. 10 units, including some cottages. TV, pool.

Cedar Glen Lodge. *$52-$75*. 6589 North Lake Blvd., Tahoe Vista; (916) 546-4281. 32 units, some cottages with kitchens. TV, phones, pool, sauna, spas, beach. Complimentary continental breakfast.

Charmey Chalet Motel. *$65-$90*. 6549 North Lake Blvd., Kings Beach; (916) 546-2529. 25 rooms, some with fireplaces and kitchenettes; TV, pool, hot tubs.

Cottonwood Lodge. *$44-$69*. Tahoe Vista; (916) 546-2220. 18 units, some with kitchens. TV, phones, pool, sauna and spas. Private beach and pier.

Crown Motel. *$45-$85*. 8200 North Lake Blvd., Kings Beach; (916) 546-3388. 39 units, including some family units and some with kitchens. TV, phones, pool, spa and beach.

Falcon Motor Lodge. *$35-$54*. 8258 North Lake Blvd., Kings Beach; (916) 546-2583. 30 units, some with lake views. TV, pool, private beach.

Franciscan Lakeside Lodge. *$65-$95*. 6944 North Lake Blvd., Tahoe Vista; (916) 546-7234. 58 units, including some lakefront cottages with fireplaces and kitchens. Private beach and pier; TV, pool.

Goldcrest Resort Motel. *$48-$65*. 8194 North Lake Blvd., Kings Beach; (916) 546-3301/(702) 831-7103. 25 rooms, some with lake views; TV, phones, pool, hot tubs.

Garni Motor Lodge. *$45-$58*. 9937 Highway 28, Kings Beach; (916) 546-3341. 100 rooms, TV, phones, pool, sauna.

Mourelatos' Lakeshore Resort. *$55-$65*. 6834 North Lake Blvd., Tahoe Vista; (916) 583-5334/(800) 553-1555. 32 rooms, some with kitchens, some lakeviews. TV, phones, private beach.

North Lake Lodge. *$40-$55*. 8716 North Lake Blvd., Kings Beach; (916) 546-2731. 20 units, most with kitchenettes. TV, hot tub.

Rustic Cottage Resort. *$50-$75*. 7449 North Lake Blvd., Tahoe Vista; (916) 546-3523. 18 cottages, all with kitchens and fireplaces; also some Japanese-style bedrooms. TV, phones.

Tahoe Sands Resort. *$60-$95*. Tahoe Vista; (916) 546-2592. 66 rooms, TV, phones, pool, hot tubs.

Stevenson's Holliday Inn. *$40-$45*. 8742 North Lake Blvd., Kings Beach; (916) 546-2269. 24 units, some with kitchens and fireplaces; also some lakefront units. TV, phones, pool, hot tubs.

Tahoya Shores Lodge. *$65-$85*. 7610 North Lake Blvd., Tahoe Vista; (916) 546-2571. 28 units, some with lake views. TV, phones, pool.

Thornley Lodge. *$40-$50*. 7630 North Lake Blvd., Tahoe Vista; (916) 546-3952. 23 units, TV, pool, spas. Located on the lake, with a private beach. Some kitchen units.

Villa Vista Resort. *$55-$115*. 6750 North Lake Blvd., Tahoe Vista; (916) 546-3333. 13 units, including a lakefront 2-bedroom cottage. TV, phones, pool.

Incline Village and Crystal Bay

All Seasons Resort. *$99+.* 807 Alder Ave., Incline Village; (702) 831-2311/(800) 322-4331. 98 condominium units with kitchens and fireplaces. TV, phones, pool, spa and weight room.

Club Tahoe. *$100+.* Northwood Blvd., Incline Village; (702) 831-5750/ (800) 527-5154. 2-bedroom condominiums with kitchens and fireplaces. TV, phones, pool, spas, sauna, exercise room, tennis and racquetball courts, deli and cocktail lounge.

The Inn at Incline. *$55-$85.* 1003 Tahoe Blvd., Incline Village; (702) 831-1052. 30 rooms, TV, phones, pool, spa, sauna.

Hyatt Lake Tahoe. *$90-$400.* Cnr. Lakeshore Blvd. and Country Club Dr., Incline Village; (702) 831-1111. 460-room, full-service hotel-casino. TV, phones; some rooms with lakeviews and fireplaces. Also sauna, jacuzzi and pool. 3 restaurants on premises.

Cal-Neva Lodge. *$70-$300.* Hwy. 28, Crystal Bay; (702) 832-4000/(800) 225-6382. 220 lakeview rooms; TV, phones, pool, health club. Also restaurant and casino.

HOW TO GET AROUND

By Bus. The North Lake Tahoe area is serviced by *TART* (Tahoe Area Regional Transit), which has regular, scheduled services between Meeks Bay and Tahoe City, between Tahoe City and the north Stateline, and the north Stateline and Incline Village. *TART* buses arrive at and depart both Meeks Bay and the Stateline on the hour, and service Tahoe City and Incline Village on the half-hour. There are several marked bus stops on West Lake Boulevard (Highway 89) and North Lake Boulevard (Highway 28). Fare is $1.00 one way. For timetables and information, call (916) 581-6365 in California, or (800) 325-TART in Nevada.

In winter, free ski shuttle buses are also available to and from many of North Lake Tahoe's ski areas, including Alpine Meadows, Squaw Valley, Northstar, Mount Rose, and Diamond Peak at Ski Incline. Call the respective ski area for a timetable and more information.

By Taxi. Four small taxi companies service the North Lake Tahoe area: *Lake Tahoe Taxi*, (916) 546-4444; *North Shore Taxi*, (916) 546-3181; *Tahoe City Cab*, (916) 583-8294; and *Truckee Taxi Co.*, (916) 587-6336.

By Car. Car rentals in the area are available at *Thrifty Rent-a-Car*, (916) 587-2588; *Hertz*, (916) 583-5967/(702) 831-4371, *Incline Village Compacts*, (702) 831-3726, and *National Car Rental System*, (916) 587-6748. Many of the car rental agencies also have four-wheel-drive vehicles, with snow tires, chains and ski-racks.

SEASONAL EVENTS

January. *Winterskol.* Scheduled for the last week of the month. Well-known week-long winter carnival hosted by the Incline Village community. Features a variety of festivities and celebrations, as well as several ski races at Diamond Peak at Ski Incline. For more information and a schedule of events, contact the Incline Village Chamber of Commerce at (702) 831-4440.

February. *Sled Dog Races.* Locally sponsored event, held at the Truckee Airport, lasting two whole days. Some 75 teams compete in three-dog and eight-dog freight categories for a $5,000 purse. For more information, contact the Truckee-Donner Chamber of Commerce at (916) 587-2757.

March. *Snowfest.* First and second weeks of the month. 10-day winter carnival, featuring a variety of ski races, fireworks, torchlight parade at Squaw Valley, crowning of a Snowfest Queen, ice sculpture competition, and several other gala happenings. For schedule of events and information, call (916) 583-7625. *Great Ski Race.* Hosted by the Tahoe Nordic Ski Center, usually scheduled for the first weekend in March. 30-kilometer cross-country ski race from Tahoe City to Truckee, claimed to be the largest race of its kind in the West, featuring over 700 racers. For more information, call (916) 583-9858.

June. *Truckee Airshow.* Last weekend of the month. Well-known Northern California airshow; events include aerobatics, historic war games, and air races; also display of vintage planes. More information on (916) 587-4119.

July. *Fourth of July.* Firework displays at the Tahoe City Commons Beach, as well as in Kings Beach and Incline Village. *Lake Tahoe Summer Music Festival.* Second and third weeks. Series of concerts by the San Francisco Chamber Orchestra. For a schedule, call (916) 583-7625. *Sand Harbor Music Festival.* Held at Sand Harbor (just south of Incline Village); fourth week. Music concerts, featuring jazz, pop and blues. Beach setting. For a schedule and more information, contact the North Tahoe Fine Arts Council, (916) 583-9048.

August. *Concours d'Elegance.* First weekend of the month. Antique boat show featuring pre-war wooden boats; hosted by the Tahoe Boat Company Marina, Tahoe City. *Shakespeare at Sand Harbor.* Annual, two-week event; series of Shakespeare plays, performed by members of professional theater companies. Beach setting. For schedule and reservations, call (916) 583-9048. *Donner Lake Bathtub Races and Regatta.* First weekend. Fun-filled carnival, centered around the annual Bathtub Races. Other events include parasailing and waterskiing demonstrations, and a boat show. (916) 587-3157. *Truckee Rodeo.* Held at the Truckee River Park in Truckee. One of the best-known rodeos in the area. More information on (916) 581-1102. *Squaw Valley Fine Arts & Crafts Festival.* Second weekend. Well-known festival, with some excellent displays of arts and crafts; also features entertainment, food concessions, and a variety of theatrical and musical presentations. More information on (916) 583-6985.

September. *Bonanza Days.* First weekend. Four-day western-style celebration featuring a variety of events, including a cow-chip throwing contest, pig races, cowboy poetry and music, a miners' and loggers' ball, chili cook-off, western dance exhibition, country-western music and old-fashioned melodrama. For a schedule and more information, call the Incline Village Visitors and Convention Bureau at (702) 832-1606. *Great Reno Balloon Race.* Second weekend. Fun-filled, colorful annual event, one of the largest of its kind in the West, featuring over 100 hot-air balloons. Held at Rancho San Rafael Park. (702) 826-1181. *Reno National Championship Air Races.* Third weekend; at the Reno Stead Airport. Four-day event, includes races in a variety of airplanes. Also formation flying, skydiving, aerobatics and air show. (702) 826-7500.

October. *Autumn Jubilee.* Scheduled for the latter part of the month. One of North Lake Tahoe's newest festivals, offering a variety of events and celebrations: Oktoberfest, food and wine tastings, firefighters' and homecoming parade, barbeque and street dance, and kite flying competitions. For a schedule, contact the Festivals Office at (916) 583-7625.

TOURS

Scenic Tours

Foremost among North Lake Tahoe's tour operators is *See Tahoe Tours* (702) 832-0713, which has tours of Lake Tahoe, Carson City and historic Virginia City, with live commentary and complimentary breakfast and lunch. Another tour operator in the area is *Safaris, Inc.* (702) 831-4657, which also has lake tours. Additionally, guided tours of North Lake Tahoe's *Historic Homes* are offered by the North Lake Tahoe Historical Society, usually in summer. For reservations and more information, call the Society at (916) 583-1762.

Scenic Flights

For sightseeing flights over Lake Tahoe and the surrounding Sierra country, contact any of the following: *Coyote Flying Services*, (916) 587-6914; *Pilot Services Corp.*, (916) 583-1710/582-1102; *Dale Aviation*, (702) 831-1358. All flights originate at the Tahoe-Truckee Airport, just southeast of Truckee. For scenic glider rides call *Soar Truckee, Inc.*, (916) 587-6702. Also, the *Cal-Vada Seaplane Base* at Homewood, 6 miles south of Tahoe City, offers aerial sightseeing tours on board Super Cub seaplanes; for more information, call (916) 525-7143.

PLACES OF INTEREST

Donner Memorial State Park and Museum. 4 miles west of Truckee on Donner Pass Road. Public park, centered around the ill-fated Donner Party families. Several short walks lead to the campsites of the Donner families, who spent the 1846-47 winter here. The park has in it the *Emigrant Monument*, built on the site of the Breen family cabin, and the *Emigrant Museum* which has some excellent exhibits from the Central Pacific Railroad days as well as picture slide shows and old photographs recounting the Donner Party ordeal. Also, nearby is the *Donner Lake*, with good boating and fishing possibilities. The museum is open daily, 10-12 and 1-4; admission 50¢. Museum phone: (916) 587-3841.

Western America Ski Sport Museum. Located near Boreal Ridge; exit off I-80. Features ski exhibits dating from 1860, including Snowshoe Thompson history and artifacts. Also some Squaw Valley Winter Olympic Games memorabilia. Open May-Oct., Wed.-Fri. 12-4, Sat. and Sun. 11-5, closed Mon.; admission free. (916) 426-3313.

Squaw Valley. 4 miles northwest of Tahoe City, off Hwy. 89. World-renowned ski resort; site of the 1960 Winter Olympic Games. Ride the *Squaw Valley Aerial Tram* to the Granite Chief restaurant perched at 8,200 feet; spectacular views enroute. Tram operates June 30-Sept. 2, 10-5.

Fanny Bridge and Outlet Gates. Located at the Tahoe City "Y" (intersection of Hwys. 89 and 28). The bridge is a summertime favorite; watch Rainbow trout in pool beneath the bridge. The dam at the Outlet Gates was built in 1910. This is also the lake's sole outlet.

Gatekeeper's Cabin. Just south of Outlet Gates, reached via the parking lot between the Truckee River Bank and Bridgetender Restaurant, off West Lake Blvd. Picturesque, hand-hewn log cabin, situated in a park-like setting, now a museum operated by North Lake Tahoe Historical Society. View artifacts and old Tahoe photographs. Open May-Oct., 11-5.

Watson's Log Cabin. In the heart of Tahoe City, on North Lake Blvd. Oldest building in the area, originally built in the 1880's as the honeymoon cottage of Robert and Stella Watson. Now houses a North Lake Tahoe Historical Society museum, with exhibits of local historic interest. Open during summer.

Tahoe City Commons Beach. Popular beach area, situated in the center of town. Site of annual Fourth of July fireworks display. Swimming and picnic areas, volleyball courts, fire pits, restrooms. Open to the public year-round.

Roundhouse Mall. Located in Tahoe City. Restored 1890's Southern Pacific Railroad building, now housing gift shops and one or two restaurants. At the front of the mall is the *Tahoe Boat Company Marina*, where antique boats can be viewed during the annual Concours d'Elegance, held in July.

Cobblestone Mall. In Tahoe City, off North Lake Blvd. Charming replica of a Bavarian Alpine Village, with a Tudor mural and clocktower. Houses some worthwhile gift shops and a cafe. Open-ended mall.

Fleur du Lac. 4 miles south of Tahoe City on Hwy 89. This is the former Henry J. Kaiser Estate, where "Godfather II" was filmed. Large grey-stone wall encircles the estate, and it is not open to the general public. It is best viewed from the lake; take a cruise on board North Lake Tahoe Cruises' *Sunrunner*, for this pauses before the estate, with a commentary on its history.

Chamber's Landing. Just past Homewood, reached via a small side road off Hwy. 89. Restored 1870's over-water clubhouse, perched on an odd-shaped pier, now operating as a cocktail bar and lounge; superb views of the lake. There is also a sandy beach here. The clubhouse is open during summer.

Sugar Pine Point State Park. Nearly 8 miles south of Tahoe City. 2,000-acre park with several enchanting walks through it. Visit the fabulous *Ehrman Mansion*, located at the end of a small side road, east off the highway (the turnoff is marked with a "picnic area" sign). The mansion is a magnificent, gabled and turreted three-story edifice, built in 1903 and billed as "the finest High Sierra summer home in California." Splendid grounds, open to the public year-round. The mansion itself is open during summer, with State Park personnel offering guided tours through it. Park fee: $3.00 per car.

D.L. Bliss State Park. Just south of Sugar Pine Point, on Hwy. 89. 957-acre park, with some wooded walks and one or two sandy beaches. Contains several interesting rock formations, including the *Balancing Rock*, located just inside the park. Also visit the *Old Lighthouse* site above *Rubicon Point* (the deepest point on Lake Tahoe's shoreline, with a 1400-foot vertical drop). Open May-Sept.

Emerald Bay State Park - Vikingsholm. See South Lake Tahoe *Places of Interest* section.

Northstar-at-Tahoe. Just over the Brockway Summit (north of Kings Beach), off Hwy. 267. 2,500-acre "model development," dating from the early 1970s. There is a ski area and golf course worth visiting here. Also features an arts and crafts fair in summer.

Kellogg Mansion. In Tahoe Vista, Hwy. 28. Picturesque stone mansion, overlooking the lake, built around 1910 as the summer home of the cereal king from Battle Creek. Now houses a French-seafood restaurant, *La Playa*.

Ponderosa Ranch. Situated at the southeast corner of Incline Village, off Hwy. 28. Rambling western theme park; site of the TV series, "Bonanza." Visit the *Cartwright Home, Mystery Mine Shaft, Ponderosa Church*, petting farm, and several western shops and museums with interesting displays of ancient firearms, carriages, wagons, and farm machinery. Also visit stables for scenic horseback rides through the Ponderosa back country. Open May-Oct., 10-6; admission $5.00 adults, $4.00 children. For information, call (702) 831-0691.

Sand Harbor Recreation Area. 2 miles south of Ponderosa Ranch, off Hwy. 28. Lovely little harbor, with sandy beaches, picnic areas, and one or two sheltered swimming areas. Also site of a Shakespeare festival and live music concerts in summer, July-Sept. The park is open year-round; day use fee, $4.00 per car.

Art Galleries. *Timberline Crafts Gallery,* 590 Lakeshore Drive, Incline Village (702) 831-2460; pottery, stained glass, blown glass, jewelry and weavings. *Lake Gallery* at Boatworks Mall, Tahoe City (916) 583-1002; fine prints of works by internationally famous artists. *Sierra Galleries,* Boatworks Mall, Tahoe City (916) 581-5111; bronze sculptures and paintings. *High Country Silver Works,* 600 N. Lake Blvd., Tahoe City (916) 583-1600; a variety of artists, material and media, with an operating jewelry studio. *The Potlatch,* 324 Ski Way, Incline Village (702) 831-2485; Indian jewelry, wood carvings, stone carvings and western art. *Lakeside Gallery,* 8636 N. Lake Blvd., Kings Beach (916) 546-3135; oils by local artists. *Artruckee,* Commercial Row, Truckee (916) 587-5189. Original paintings and sculpture, serigraphs and posters.

LAKE CRUISES

The *Sunrunner*, operated by *North Tahoe Cruises* offers daily scenic and historic cruises along the west shore, May-Oct. The *Sunrunner* departs from the Tahoe Boat Company Marina in Tahoe City, and includes on its itinerary the fabled Fleur du Lac estate where the movie "Godfather II" was filmed on location. Tour cost: $12.00 adults, $5.00 children. Also private charters are available for weddings, parties, conventions and other occasions. For reservations and information, call (916) 583-0141.

Other smaller boats are also available for charter at many of the area's marinas.

RAFTING

Rafting is available on the Truckee River, along a 4-mile section between Tahoe City and River Ranch (near the Alpine Meadows Road turnoff). Currently there are four commercial rafting companies operating on the river: *Mountain Air Sports*, (916) 583-5606; *Truckin on the Truckee*, (916) 581-0123; *Fanny Bridge Raft Rentals*, (916) 583-3021; and *Truckee River Rafting Center*, (916) 583-RAFT. All the operators are located just to the west of the Tahoe City Y, on River Road (Hwy. 89). Raft rental cost is around $15.00 for adults and $10.00 for children, and the rafting companies operate shuttle buses to ferry rafters back to the point of origin.

FISHING

(A valid California or Nevada fishing license is required to fish in the lake. For a license and local fishing regulations, contact the *California Department of Fish and Game*, Box 73, Tahoe City, (916) 583-3325.)

Fishing Hot Spots

Rubicon Bay and Meeks Bay. ½ mile out from the shore. Kokanee salmon are plentiful in summer.

Chambers Run. Opposite Chambers Landing, just north from Sugar Pine Point. Deeplining at depths of 100-300 feet.

McKinney Bay. Out from the Homewood shoreline. Mackinaw and Browns abound.

Kaspian Area. Just north of Kaspian Beach. Deepline for Mackinaw trout.

Tahoe Tavern Hole. Opposite the Tahoe Tavern Properties, ½ mile south of the Tahoe City shoreline. Mackinaw are abundant.

Tahoe Flats. 1½ miles out from the Lake Tahoe Dam at Tahoe City. Excellent trolling at depths of 25-30 feet.

Agate Bay. Out from the Tahoe Vista and Kings Beach shorelines. The entire bay is favored for deepline fishing at depths of 100-200 feet.

Stateline Point. Just beneath the peninsular tract of Crystal Bay. Deepline.

Crystal Bay. Along the Incline Village shoreline, not too far out from the shore. Topline is suggested for Rainbows and Browns.

Sand Harbor. South from Incline Village. Inshore fishing is excellent along rocky points.

Secret Harbor. 4 miles south of Sand Harbor. Trolling at depths of 20-70 feet, close to the shore.

Truckee River. Almost the entire river provides for excellent fly fishing.

Fishing Guides

Year-round fishing charters and guide services are available at the following: *King Fish*, Tahoe City, (916) 525-5360; *Mickey's Guide Service*, Tahoe City, (916) 583-4602; *Hooker for Hire*, Tahoe City, (916) 525-5654.

HIKING TRAILS

(Wilderness permits are required for some of the trails in the area. For a permit, maps and additional information, contact the Lake Tahoe Basin Management Unit, 870 Emerald Bay Road, South Lake Tahoe; (916) 573-2600.)

West Shore Area

Meeks Bay Trail. Across from Meeks Bay Resort, a dirt road leads to the trailhead, which is situated some 1½ miles southwest of the resort; this is a popular entry point for the Desolation Wilderness area. The trail winds south through the wilderness, past a series of little lakes—including Genevieve Lake, Crag Lake, Shadow Lake, Stony Ridge Lake and Rubicon Lake. 4.6-mile trail; allow a full day.

Sugar Pine Point Nature Trail. A 1½-mile-loop, the trail starts out near the Ehrman Mansion in the Sugar Pine Point State Park, then winds through the Sugar Pine Point Natural Preserve. Takes approximately 1 hour.

General Creek Trail. This is a particularly enchanting trail that begins at the General Creek Campground parking area, west of Highway 89, and wanders alongside of the General Creek, tracing a loop. Stream crossings and wooded picnic areas are encountered along the way, as well as some idyllic scenery. The loop is 5½ miles, expected to take 5 hours.

General Phipps Cabin Trail. The trail begins at the Sugar Pine Point picnic area, just off Highway 89, and leads to the site of the Indian fighter General Phipps' cabin. It is a ½-mile trail, expected to take 30 minutes.

Twin Peaks Trail. Look for the trailhead on Ward Creek Boulevard, at the back of Pineland. The trail follows Ward Creek much of the way, ending at Twin Peaks; the summit offers spectacular views of Lake Tahoe. Allow a full day for this 5-mile trail.

Paige Meadows Trail. The trail is accessed by way of the Twin Peaks trailhead on Ward Creek Boulevard. It is a short, steep trail, leading to the unspoilt Paige Meadows, where a variety of wildflowers can be observed. 1 mile, 1 hour each way.

Five Lakes Trail. The trailhead is situated on the right side of Alpine Meadows Road, past Deer Park Drive, some 2 miles in from Highway 89. The trail is moderately steep, and leads to a group of five tiny lakes. 2 miles, 2½ hours each way.

Lake Tahoe State Park Area

Tunnel Creek Station Trail. The trailhead is located opposite Hidden Beach (a mile south of Ponderosa Ranch), just off Highway 28. A 1½-mile trail leads to the ruins of the old Tunnel Creek Station; views enroute are breathtaking. Allow approximately 4 hours for the round trip.

Twin Lakes Trail. The trail begins opposite Hidden Beach, and journeys southeast to two tiny, adjoining lakes. 5-mile round trip.

Spooner Lake Trail. This trail is also accessed from the Hidden Beach trailhead. The 16-mile trail leads south to Spooner Lake. The length of the trail warrants a pick-up at the Spooner Lake end.

North Canyon Trail. Parking is off the highway, adjacent to Spooner Lake. The trail winds north from the lake, through the beautiful North Canyon to Marlette Lake—a modest-sized lake which, during the 19th century, provided water for the V-flumes transporting logs to Carson Valley. 10 miles of trail; allow a full day.

Granite Chief Area

Situated northwest of Squaw Valley, this 40,000-acre backcountry recreation area boasts a bonanza of hiking trails; the area has been set aside exclusively for hikers and horseback riders. Contact the U.S. Forest Service for information on the area's trails; call (916) 583-3642 or (916) 587-3558.

BICYCLING

North Lake Tahoe has more than 50 miles of bike trails, both along the north and west shores, as well as along the Truckee River, northwest of Tahoe City. Bike rentals are available at several locations throughout the area, including the following: *Olympic Bike Shop,* 620 North Lake Blvd., Tahoe City, (916) 581-2500; *Wray's Rentals,* 315 West Lake Blvd., Tahoe City, (916) 581-3030; *Cyclepaths,* 1785 West Lake Blvd., Sunnyside, (916) 581-1171; *Tahoe Gear,* 5095 West Lake Blvd., Homewood, (916) 525-5233; *Timbers Bicycles,* 2911 Lake Forest Road, Lake Forest, (916) 581-4141; *Kings Beach Bicycles,* 8626 North Lake Blvd., Kings Beach, (916) 546-3664; *Sierra Cycle Works,* 8106 North Lake Blvd., Kings Beach, (916) 546-7992; *The Outdoorsman,* 910 Tahoe Blvd., Incline Village, (702) 831-0446; *Village Bicycles,* 800 Tahoe Blvd., Incline Village, (702) 831-3537; *Paco's Truckee River Bicycles,* 11400 Donner Pass Road, Truckee, (916) 587-5561; and *Mountain Bikes Unlimited,* 10200 Commercial Row, Truckee, (916) 587-7711.

BEACHES AND PICNIC AREAS

D.L. Bliss State Park. Off Highway 89, north of Emerald Bay; look for sign. Picnic area, campsites, fire pits, restrooms, and parking; dogs on leash only.

Meeks Bay Resort. On Highway 89, 10 miles south of Tahoe City. Picnic area, swimming, aquacycle and paddleboat rentals, volleyball court, ice-cream and hot-dog stand, gift shop, restroom facilities. Also full-service marina. Limited parking; parking fee: $3.00 per car.

Sugar Pine Point State Park-Ehrman Mansion. Off Highway 89, just north of Meeks Bay. Facilities include picnic area, restrooms, pier, swimming, water ski area, boat docking and parking; parking fee: $3.00 per car.

Chamber's Landing Beach. Off Highway 89, just south of Homewood. Volleyball court, swimming, lifeguard; also cocktail lounge and bar.

Kaspian Picnic Area and Beach. Off Highway 89, 3 miles south of Tahoe City. Picnic area, swimming, fire pits, and parking are available.

William Kent Beach. Just off Highway 89, 2 miles south of Tahoe City. Picnic area, swimming, lifeguard, fire pits, and restroom facilities; limited parking.

Tahoe City Commons Beach. In the heart of Tahoe City, just past the fire station. Picnic area, swimming, lifeguard, fire pits, grass area, volleyball courts, restrooms, and limited parking.

Tahoe Recreation Area Beach. Off Highway 28, ½ mile northeast of Tahoe City. Picnic area, swimming, fire pits, restrooms.

Lake Forest Beach. 1½ miles northeast of Tahoe City, at the foot of Tamarack Street (off Lake Forest Road). Picnic area, boat ramp, volleyball courts, swimming, fire pits, restrooms, and limited parking.

Patton Beach. Off Highway 28, just north of Carnelian Bay. Picnic area; and parking.

Agatam Beach. Also off Highway 28, in Tahoe Vista. Picnic area, restrooms; and parking.

Moondunes Beach. At the bottom of National Avenue (off Highway 28) in Tahoe Vista. A sandy beach, with excellent swimming facilities.

Secline Beach. In Kings Beach, at the foot of Secline Street. Parking is available off Highway 28.

Kings Beach Recreation Area. At the foot of Coon Street, in downtown Kings Beach. Picnic area is at the eastern end of the beach; restrooms, a boat ramp, volleyball courts and parking, too, are available.

Hidden Beach. 2 miles south from the Ponderosa Ranch, just off Highway 28. Offers swimming and hiking.

Nevada State Park at Sand Harbor. 4 miles south of Incline Village (or 2 miles south of Hidden Beach), just off Highway 28. Restrooms, boat ramp, swimming, lifeguard, and parking; a $4.00 fee is charged for parking.

CAMPGROUNDS

D.L. Bliss Campground. Alongside Highway 89, north of Emerald Bay. 168 sites, restrooms, swimming, hiking and fishing; 10-day limit. Reservations (916) 525-7277.

Meeks Bay Resort. On Highway 89, 10 miles south of Tahoe City; (916) 525-7242. 28 sites, rental cabins, restrooms, store, boat ramp, swimming, no pets. No day limit.

D.L. Bliss Campground. Alongside Highway 89, north of Emerald Bay; (916) 525-7277. 168 sites, restrooms, swimming, hiking and fishing; 10-day limit.

General Creek Campground. On Highway 89, 9 miles south of Tahoe City; (916) 525-7982. 175 sites, restrooms, showers, swimming, hiking and fishing; 10-day limit. Open year-round.

Kaspian Recreation Area Campground. On Highway 89, 3 miles south of Tahoe City; (916) 573-2600. 10 sites, restrooms, swimming, hiking; 7-day limit.

William Kent Campground. Just off Highway 89, 2 miles south of Tahoe City; (916) 583-3642. 95 sites, restrooms, beach, swimming, fishing; 7-day limit.

Tahoe State Recreation Area. On Highway 28, just north of Tahoe City; (916) 583-3074. 39 sites, restrooms, showers, and fishing; 10-day limit.

Lake Forest Campground. On Highway 28, 1½ miles northeast of Tahoe City; (916) 583-5544. 21 sites, restrooms, showers, boat ramp, beach, swimming, fishing and hiking; no pets. 14-day limit.

Silver Creek Campground. On Highway 89 (on the Truckee River), 7 miles north of Tahoe City; (916) 587-3558. 30 sites, restrooms, swimming, fishing, hiking and riding; 14-day limit.

Goose Meadows Campground. On Highway 89 (on the Truckee River), 9 miles north of Tahoe City; (916) 587-3558. 30 sites, restrooms, swimming, fishing, hiking; 14-day limit.

Granite Flat Campground. On Highway 89 (on the river), 2 miles south of Truckee; (916) 587-3558. 75 sites, restrooms, swimming, fishing, and hiking; 14-day limit.

Donner Memorial Campground. 2 miles west of Truckee, off Donner Pass Road in the Donner Memorial State Park; (916) 587-3841. 125 sites, restrooms, showers, boat ramp, swimming, fishing, hiking and riding; 10-day limit.

WATER SPORTS

Marinas

Meeks Bay Marina. 10 miles south of Tahoe City, off Highway 89; (916) 525-7242. Slips, boat ramp, gas supplies, rentals, snack bar. Open through summer. $6.00 in, $6.00 out.

High & Dry Marina. Off Highway 89, 6 miles south of Tahoe City; (916) 525-5966. Buoys, forklift launching, gas supplies, repairs, rentals, sales and storage. Open summers. $15.00 in, $15.00 out.

Obexer's Marina. Off Highway 89, in Homewood; (916) 525-7962. Slips, buoys, boat ramp, gas supplies, repairs, rentals, storage, snack bar. Open year-round. $5.00 in, $5.00 out.

Sunnyside Resort and Marina. 1½ miles south of Tahoe City, off Highway 89; (916) 583-9420. Slips, buoys, forklift, hoist, gas supplies, repairs, rentals, storage and restaurant. Open through summer. $25.00 each way.

Tahoe Boat Company Marina. In Tahoe City, at the front of the Round-house Mall; (916) 583-5567. Slips, buoys, gas supplies, repairs, rentals, sales, storage, snack bar. Open through summer. $25.00 each way.

Sierra Boat Company. Off Highway 28, 1½ miles south of Kings Beach; (916) 546-2552. Slips, buoys, gas supplies, repairs, rentals, storage. Open year-round. $20.00 one way.

Tahoe Vista Marina. Off Highway 28, Tahoe Vista; (916) 546-3185. Slips, buoys, gas supplies, restaurant, and cocktail lounge; no launches. Open summers.

North Tahoe Marina. Also off Highway 28, next to the Tahoe Vista Marina; (916) 546-8248. Slips, buoys, hoist, boat ramp, gas supplies, repairs, rentals, sales, storage, snack bar. Open through summer. $18.00 one way.

Public Launching Ramps. Public boat-launching ramps are available at the following locations in the North Lake Tahoe area: *Lake Forest*, 1 mile north of Tahoe City; at the bottom end of *Coon Street*, in Kings Beach; and at *Sand Harbor*, roughly 3½ miles south of Incline Village. Fees at the public launching ramps are around $5.00 round trip.

Water Skiing

High Sierra Water Ski School and Sailing Center. Sunnyside Marina, 1850 West Lake Blvd., Sunnyside; (916) 583-7417. Water skiing lessons and equipment rentals; also sailing lessons, sailboat rentals and powerboat rentals.

Jet Ski Rentals

Tahoe Boat Co. Roundhouse Mall, North Lake Blvd., Tahoe City; (916) 583-5571. Jet ski rentals available.

Tahoe Family Center. 8040 North Lake Blvd., Kings Beach; (916) 546-2977. Jet ski rentals; also raft and rubber boat rentals.

Mountain Lake Adventures. Incline Village; (702) 831-4202. Jet ski rentals; also pedal boats, canoes, kayaks and windsurfers.

Tahoe Water Adventures. Lakehouse Pizza Pier, Grove Street, Tahoe City; (916) 583-3225. Jet ski, power boat and canoe rentals.

High Sierra Boat Rentals. Homewood; (916) 525-5589. Jet ski and power boat rentals; also pedal boats.

Lakeside Boat & Sail. North Tahoe Beach Center, Kings Beach; (916) 546-5889/546-2566. Jet skis, pedal boats, canoes, kayaks, sailboats, sailboards and aquacycles.

GOLF

Incline Executive Golf Course. Off Wilson Way in Incline Village; (702) 832-1150. 18 holes, 3440 yards, 58 Par; green fee: $40.00/with cart (cart mandatory). A pro shop and a snack bar are available on the premises.

Incline Championship Golf Course. On Fairway Boulevard in Incline Village, just off Northwood Boulevard; (702) 832-1144. 18 holes, 7120 yards, 72 Par; green fee: $75.00/with cart (cart mandatory). Facilities: pro shop, driving range, bar and snack bar.

Old Brockway Golf Club. Wedged between Highways 28 and 267 in Kings Beach; (916) 546-9909. 9 holes, 3100 yards, 35 Par; green fee: $17.00/9 holes, $25.00/18 holes. Carts, pro shop, driving range, and restaurant.

Tahoe City Golf Course. In Tahoe City, behind the Bank of America; (916) 583-1516. 9 holes, 2700 yards, 33 Par; green fee: $15.00/9 holes, $20.00/18 holes. Carts, pro shop, putting green, restaurant.

Northstar-at-Tahoe Golf Course. Off Highway 267, 6 miles north of Kings Beach; (916) 587-0290. 18 holes, 6897 yards, 72 Par; green fee: $35.00/18 holes, $20.00/twilight. Carts, pro shop, driving range, restaurant.

Ponderosa Golf Course. On Highway 267, 1 mile south of Truckee; (916) 587-3501. 9 holes, 3000 yards, 36 Par; green fee: $20.00/18 holes, $13.00/9 holes. Carts, pro shop, snack bar.

Tahoe Donner Golf and Country Club. On Northwoods Boulevard, 2 miles west of Truckee; (916) 587-9440. 18 holes, 7000 yards, 72 Par; green fee: $36.00/weekday, $45.00/weekend, $19.00/twilight. Carts, pro shop, driving range, restaurant and bar.

Miniature Golf Courses

Magic Carpet Miniature Golf. On Highway 28 in Carnelian Bay; (916) 546-4279. Two courses available, one 19 holes and the other 28 holes.

Boberg's Mini-Golf. On Highway 28 in Kings Beach; (916) 546-3196. Two 19-hole courses available.

TENNIS

Sugar Pine Point State Park-Ehrman Mansion. Just off Highway 89, 8½ miles south of Tahoe City. 1 court; no lights.

Kilner Park. 2 miles south of Tahoe City, off Highway 89. 2 courts; lights. Phone (916) 583-5544.

Granlibakken. Just south of Tahoe City, at the end of Tonopah Drive (off Highway 89). 8 courts; no lights. Private lessons. Phone (916) 583-4242.

Squaw Valley Tennis Club. In Squaw Valley, at the end of Squaw Valley Road (off Highway 89). 4 courts; no lights. Private lessons. Phone (916) 583-0035.

Tahoe Lake School. On Grove Street in Tahoe City. 2 courts; lights.

North Tahoe High School. Just north of Tahoe City, on Polaris Road in Highlands. 4 courts; lights.

North Tahoe Regional Park. In Tahoe Vista, at the end of National Avenue. 5 courts; lights. Phone (916) 546-7248.

Kings Beach Elementary School. In Kings Beach, between Wolf Street and Steelhead Avenue. 2 courts; no lights.

Incline High School. On Village Boulevard in Incline Village. 4 courts; no lights.

Lakeside Tennis Club. In Incline Village, just off Highway 28. 13 courts; no lights. Private lessons. Phone (702) 831-5258.

HORSEBACK RIDING

Area Stables

Alpine Meadows Stables, 4 miles north of Tahoe City, off Highway 89; (916) 583-3905. Guided scenic mountain rides.

Squaw Valley Stables, Squaw Valley Road; (916) 583-0419. Guided trail rides, breakfast rides, pony rides, lessons.

Northstar Stables, at the Northstar Resort on Highway 267; (916) 562-1230. Guided trail rides, breakfast and dinner rides, pony rides, lessons.

Ponderosa Ranch, on Highway 28 at the southeast corner of Incline Village; (702) 831-2154. Guided trail rides, breakfast and dinner rides.

Cold Stream Corral, Cold Stream Road, Donner Lake; (916) 587-4121. Guided trail rides, evening BBQ rides, fishing and pack trips.

WINTER SPORTS

Downhill Ski Areas

Alpine Meadows. 7 miles northwest of Tahoe City, at the end of Alpine Meadows Road (off Highway 89). Elevations: top 8700 feet, base 6840 feet; vertical drop 1730 feet. Facilities: 13 lifts, lessons, rentals, snack bar, restaurant, bar, and shuttle bus. Lift prices: $35.00/adults, $12.00/children; half day: $24.00/adults, $8.00/children. Phone (916) 583-4232/583-6914.

Diamond Peak at Ski Incline. Ski Way, Incline Village. Elevations: top 8540 feet, base 6700 feet, vertical drop 1840 feet. Facilities: 7 lifts, lessons, rentals, snack bar, restaurant. Lift prices: $28.00/adults, $12.00/children; half day: $19.00/adults, $10.00/children. Phone (702) 832-1122/831-3211.

Boreal Ridge. 10 miles west of Truckee, just off I-80 (take Castle Peak exit). Elevations: top 7800 feet, base 7200 feet, vertical drop 600 feet. Facilities: 9 lifts, night skiing, lessons, rentals, snack bar and restaurant. Lift prices: $25.00/ adults, $14.00 children; half day: $18.00 adults, $12.00/children. Phone (916)

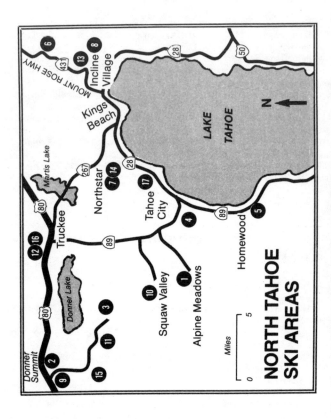

NORTH TAHOE SKI AREAS

Downhill Ski Areas -
1) Alpine Meadows
2) Boreal Ridge
3) Donner Ski Ranch
4) Granlibakken
5) Homewood Ski
6) Mount Rose
7) Northstar-at-Tahoe
8) Ski Incline/Diamond Peak
9) Soda Springs
10) Squaw Valley U.S.A.
11) Sugar Bowl
12) Tahoe Donner

Nordic Ski Areas -
13) Diamond Peak Cross-Country Center
14) Northstar Nordic Center
15) Royal Gorge
16) Tahoe Donner Nordic Center
17) Tahoe Nordic

426-3666/426-3663.

Donner Ski Ranch. West of Truckee; take Soda Springs exit off I-80, then 3½ miles down old Highway 40. Elevations: top 7960 feet, base 7135 feet, vertical drop 825 feet. Facilities: 4 lifts, lessons, rentals, child care, shuttle bus, snack bar and restaurant. Lift prices: $22.00/adults, $10.00 children; half day: $18.00/adults, $10.00 children. Phone (916) 426-3635.

Granlibakken. Just south of Tahoe City, at the end of Tonopah Drive (off Highway 89). Elevations: top 6610 feet, base 6330 feet, vertical drop 280 feet. Facilities: 2 lifts, lessons, rentals, snack bar. Lift prices: $10.00 adults, $6.00/children; half day: $6.00/adults, $4.00/children. Phone (916) 583-6203/583-9896.

Homewood. On Highway 89, 6 miles south of Tahoe City. Elevations: top 7880 feet, base 6230 feet, vertical drop 1650 feet. Facilities: 9 lifts, lessons, rentals, child care, restaurant and snack bar. Lift prices: $27.00/adults, $9.00/children; half day: $20.00/adults, $6.00/children. Phone (916) 525-7256.

Mount Rose. 10 miles north of Incline Village, on Mount Rose Highway (Route 431). Elevations: top 9700 feet, base 8250 feet, vertical drop 1450 feet. Facilities: 8 lifts, lessons, rentals, bar, snack bar and restaurant. Lift prices: $27.00/adults, $10/children; half day: $21.00/adults, $7.00/children. Phone (702) 849-0704/849-0706.

Northstar-at-Tahoe. Just off Highway 267, 6½ miles southeast of Truckee. Elevations: top 8600 feet, base 6400 feet, vertical drop 2200 feet. Facilities: 10 lifts and 1 gondola, NASTAR races, lessons, rentals, day lodge, child care, store, snack bar, restaurant, and shuttle bus. Lift prices $33.00/adults, $14.00/children; half day: $24.00/adults, $10.00/children. Phone (916) 562-1010/562-1330.

Soda Springs. West of Truckee; on old Highway 40, near Soda Springs exit off I-80. Elevations: top 7352 feet, base 6700 feet, vertical drop 652 feet. Facilities: 3 lifts, snowboarding, lessons and rentals. Lift prices: $20.00/adults, $11.00/children; half day: $11.00/adults, $9.00/children. Phone (916) 426-3666.

Squaw Valley U.S.A. 8 miles northwest of Tahoe City, at the end of Squaw Valley Road (off Highway 89). Elevations: top 8900 feet, base 6200 feet, vertical drop 2700 feet. Facilities: 30 lifts, 1 gondola, 1 tram. Lessons, rentals, child care, snack bar, restaurants, and shuttle bus. Lift prices: $35.00/adults, $5.00/children; half day: $24.00/adults, $5.00/children. Phone (916) 583-6985/583-6955.

Sugar Bowl. West of Truckee, take Soda Springs exit off I-80, then onto old Highway 40. Elevations: top 8383 feet, base 6881 feet, vertical drop 1502 feet. Facilities: 8 lifts and 1 gondola, night skiing, lessons, rentals, sleigh rides, snack bar and restaurant. Lift prices: $29.00/adults, $14.00/children; half day: $20.00/adults, $11.00/children. Phone (916) 426-3651/426-3847.

Tahoe Donner. 2½ miles northwest of Truckee, off Donner Pass Road. Elevations: top 7350 feet, base 6750 feet, vertical drop 600 feet. Facilities: 3 lifts, lessons, rentals, snack bar and restaurant. Lift prices: $18.00/adults, $10.00/children; half day: $14.00/adults, $8.00/children. Phone (916) 587-9444/587-9494.

Nordic Ski Areas

Clare Tappen Lodge. Old U.S. 40, Soda Springs. 8 kilometers of groomed trails, lodge. Trail fee: $4.00. Phone (916) 426-3632.

Diamond Peak Cross Country. Mt. Rose Hwy, Incline Village. 30 kilometers of groomed trails, snack bar, shuttle bus. Trail fee: $9.00/adults, $6.00 children. Phone (702) 832-1255.

Northstar Nordic Center. Off Highway 267, 6½ miles south of Truckee. 45 kilometers of groomed trails; tours, lodge, restaurant, child care. Trail fee: $10.00/adults, $5.00/children. Phone (916) 562-1010/562-1330.

Royal Gorge. A mile from I-80, at the Soda Springs exit. 317 kilometers of groomed trails; tours, lessons, rentals, lodge and restaurant. Trail fee: $14.50/adults, $8.50/children. Phone (916) 426-3871.

Tahoe Donner Nordic Center. West of Truckee; ½ mile from I-80, off old Highway 40. 65 kilometers of groomed trails; tours, lodge. Trail fee: $11.50/adults, $7.50/children. Phone (916) 587-9494/587-9484.

Tahoe Nordic. Off Highway 28, 2½ miles northeast of Tahoe City. 65 kilometers of groomed trails; tours, lessons, rentals, day lodge. Trail fee: $10.00/adults, $4.00/children. Phone (916) 583-9858.

Wilderness Cross-Country Ski Areas

Sugar Pine Point State Park. The trailhead is located at the State Park Ranger Station, just off Highway 89 (½ mile south of Tahoma).

Blackwood Creek. 2 miles south of Sunnyside, a forest service road branches off Highway 89 and leads to the trailhead, some 2½ miles in from the highway.

Paige Meadows. 2 miles south of Tahoe City; take Pine Avenue off Highway 89, then right on Tahoe Park Heights Drive and left on Silvertip Drive. The trailhead is located at the end of Silvertip.

Pole Creek. 9 miles north of Tahoe City, off Highway 89. The trailhead is across the street from Big Chief Lodge.

Snowmobiling

Snowmobile rentals are available at some of the area golf courses. In addition, snowmobile touring is offered by the following operators in the North Lake Tahoe area: *TC Sno Mo's* , Tahoe City, (916) 583-1516/(916) 581-3906; *Snowmobiling Unlimited*, Tahoe City, (916) 583-5858/(916) 546-4222; Mountain Lake Adventures, Tahoe City, (916) 583-9131; and Mountain Lake Adventures, Incline Village, (702) 831-4202.

Snow Play Areas

Snow play areas and sled hills open to the public can be found at the following North Lake Tahoe locations: *Granlibakken Ski Area,* ½ mile south of Tahoe City; *North Tahoe Regional Park,* at the end of National Avenue (off Highway 28) in Tahoe Vista; and *Boreal Ski Area,* 10 miles west of Truckee off Interstate 80. The *Granlibakken* and *Boreal* snow play areas have saucer rentals, and charge an admission fee, $3.00 and $5.00, respectively; the *North Tahoe Regional Park* area is free, but has no equipment rentals.

RESTAURANTS

(Restaurant prices—based on full course dinner, excluding drinks, tax and tips—are categorized as follows: *Deluxe*, over $30; *Expensive*, $20-$30; *Moderate*, $10-$20; *Inexpensive*, under $10.)

Alpenhaus. *Expensive.* Highway 89, Tahoma; (916) 525-5000. Alpine country inn, specializing in California and European cuisine. Also family-style Basque dinners, and oompa accordian music. Extensive wine list; cocktail bar. Open for breakfast, lunch and dinner daily. Dinner reservations suggested.

Azzara's. *Moderate.* At the Raley's Center in Incline Village; (702) 831-0346. Italian restaurant, featuring veal, seafood, and poultry dishes; also homemade pasta. Dinners from 5 p.m., Tues.-Sun. Reservations suggested.

Bacchi's Inn. *Moderate.* 2905 Lake Forest Rd.; (916) 583-3324. Established Italian restaurant, owned and operated by the same family for three generations. Great family-style dinners, generous portions. Bacchi's Minestrone Soup is famous the world over, featured in several gourmet magazines. Dinners daily. Reservations recommended.

Bohn House. *Expensive.* 8160 North Lake Blvd., Kings Beach; (916) 546-5814. Traditional continental cuisine. Also seafood, steak and pasta dishes. Homemade desserts. Breakfast, lunch and dinner, Thurs.-Tues. Reservations recommended.

Captain Jon's. *Deluxe.* Located at the Tahoe Vista Marina, Hwy. 28, Tahoe Vista; (916) 546-4819. French-country seafood, in lakeside setting. Among the favorites are Poached Salmon and Roast Duck with Blueberry or Oyster Sauce; also worthwhile are the seafood salads and fresh fruit daiquiries. Daily specials; extensive wine list. Dinners from 6 p.m., Tues.-Sun. Reservations required.

Christy Hill. *Expensive-Deluxe.* 115 Grove St.; (916) 583-8551. Long-standing Tahoe institution, specializing in California cuisine. Homemade chocolate mousse desserts. Lakefront setting. Open for lunch and dinner. Reservations required.

Col. Clair's. *Moderate.* North Lake Blvd., Tahoe Vista; (916) 546-7358. Cajun and Creole specialties; homemade soups. Also traditional Southern desserts. Reservations recommended.

El Toro Bravo. *Inexpensive-Moderate.* West end of Commercial Row, Truckee; (916) 587-3557. Authentic Mexican cooking. Also combination dinners and seafood specialties. Outdoor bar and patio. Open for lunch and dinner daily.

Emma Murphy's. *Moderate-Expensive.* 425 North Lake Blvd.; (916) 583-6939. Steaks, seafood, pasta and sushi. Live music. Open for lunch and dinner daily; champagne brunch on Sundays.

Gar Woods. *Moderate-Expensive.* 5000 North Lake Blvd., Carnelian Bay; (916) 546-3366. Lakeside restaurant, featuring Old Tahoe, nautical decor. Seafood and grilled specialties. Open for lunch and dinner daily, also Sunday buffet brunch.

Hacienda Del Lago. *Inexpensive-Moderate.* Boatworks Mall (upstairs), 760 North Lake Blvd.; (916) 583-0358. Popular Mexican restaurant, with cocktail lounge and deck overlooking lake. Multi-flavored margaritas. Dinner daily.

Hobee's. *Moderate.* Boatworks Mall, Tahoe City; (916) 581-1166. Country-style health-food restaurant, with extensive, varied menu, featuring tofu dishes, black bean chili, boneless-chicken burgers, soups, sandwiches, organic omelettes, and Mexican food. Also herbal and cinnamon orange tea. Lakeviews, sundeck. Open for breakfast and lunch daily, dinner Fri.-Sun.

Hugo's Rotisserie. *Expensive.* At the Hyatt Lake Tahoe; (702) 831-1111.

Elegant lakeside restaurant, serving primarily American fare. House specialty is spit-roasted Five Star Duckling. Also salad bar and dessert bar; and cocktail lounge. Open for dinner daily. Reservations recommended.

Jake's on the Lake. *Expensive.* Boatworks Mall, 760 North Lake Blvd.; (916) 583-0188. Lakefront restaurant, featuring fine, fresh seafood. Daily specials. Open for dinner; reservations advised.

La Chiminee. *Deluxe.* 8504 North Lake Blvd., Kings Beach; (916) 546-4322. Small, intimate restaurant, featuring classic French cooking. Open for dinner, reservations recommended.

La Playa. *Deluxe.* Highway 28, Tahoe Vista; (916) 546-5903. Well-known French-country seafood restaurant. Housed in the historic, native-stone Kellogg Mansion, overlooking the lake. Reservations recommended.

Left Bank Restaurant. *Expensive.* 10096 Commercial Row, Truckee; (916) 587-4694. Gourmet seafood restaurant. Open for lunch and dinner daily; also Sunday brunch. Reservations recommended.

Le Petit Pier. *Deluxe.* 7252 North Lake Blvd., Tahoe Vista; (916) 546-4464. Acknowledged as one of the finest French restaurants in California, and with a splendid lakefront setting. Specialties are lamb and pheasant dishes. Open for dinner. Reservations required.

OB's Pub and Restaurant. *Moderate-Expensive.* Commercial Row, Truckee; (916) 587-4164. Seafood, steaks, pasta, prime rib and poultry; daily specials. Open for lunch and dinner, breakfast on weekends.

Pfeifer House. *Moderate-Expensive.* Hwy. 89, ½ mile west of Tahoe City; (916) 583-3102. Excellent European dishes; large portions. House specialty is Roast Duckling in Orange Sauce. Dinners from 6 p.m. daily (except Tues.). Reservations recommended.

The Pines. *Deluxe.* At Hyatt Lake Tahoe, Incline Village; (702) 831-1111. Well-appointed restaurant with contemporary decor, specializing in international cuisine, and seafood. Open for dinner, and Sunday brunch. Reservations recommended.

River Ranch. *Moderate-Expensive.* Hwy. 89 at Alpine Meadows; (916) 583-4264. Historic lodge in lovely, on-the-river setting. Roast Duck Montmorency specialty; also seafood and veal preparations. Vintage wines by the glass. Open for dinner daily; reservations recommended.

Rosie's Cafe. *Moderate.* 571 North Lake Blvd., Tahoe City; (916) 583-8504. A local favorite, serving sandwiches, salads, burgers. Full bar. Open for breakfast, lunch and dinner.

Schaffer's Mill. *Expensive.* At Northstar, off Highway 267; (916) 562-1015. Long-established restaurant in historic setting, featuring creating American fare, prepared with the freshest ingredients. Live jazz on Sundays. Open for breakfast, lunch and dinner daily during winter, dinner and Sunday brunch in summer. Reservations suggested.

Schweizer Haus. *Expensive.* 120 Country Club Drive, Incline Village; (702) 831-4694. Established European restaurant, serving traditional Swiss and German preparations, including Wiener Schnitzel and Sauerbraten; also fondues. Open for lunch and dinner Wed.-Mon. Reservations recommended.

Soule Domain. *Moderate-Expensive.* 9983 Cove Ave., Kings Beach; (916) 546-7529. Charming little restaurant, housed in a log cabin. Specializing in California cuisine, and pasta. Dinner daily. Reservations suggested.

Sunnyside Restaurant. *Expensive.* At the Sunnyside Lodge, 1850 West Lake Blvd., Sunnyside (2 miles south of Tahoe City); (916) 583-7200. Well-regarded Tahoe City restaurant, housed in delightful, rebuilt lodge. Serves primarily seafood and salads; also sushi bar. Lakeside deck for outdoor dining. Open for lunch and dinner daily, brunch on weekends.

Swiss Lakewood Restaurant. *Expensive.* 5055 West Lake Blvd., Homewood (6 miles south of Tahoe City); (916) 525-5211. Charming European lodge, serving fine Swiss and Continental cuisine. Open for dinner, Tues.-Sun.;

reservations recommended.

Tahoe House. *Expensive.* 625 West Lake Blvd. (½ mile south of Tahoe City); (916) 583-1384. Swiss and California cuisine; seafood entrees, home-made pastas, freshly-baked bread and pastry desserts. Warm, knotty-pine decor. Dinners from 5 p.m. daily. Reservations advised.

Water Wheel Restaurant. *Moderate.* 115 West Lake Blvd., Tahoe City; (916) 583-4404. Authentic Mandarin and Szechwan cuisine. Riverside setting. Open for dinner, Tues.-Sun.

Wildflower Cafe. *Moderate.* 869 Tahoe Blvd., Incline Village; (702) 831-8072. Casual cafe, featuring American fare. Open for breakfast and lunch daily.

Wolfdale's. *Expensive.* 640 North Lake Blvd.; (916) 583-5700. Creative California seafood. Lake views. Open for dinner daily; lunch in summer. Reservations suggested.

CASINO

ROULETTE

Roulette is one of the most exciting casino games, and also one of the simplest forms of gambling. It comprises, basically, a spinning roulette wheel and a small white ball. Each betting cycle begins with the dealer spinning the ball in the opposite direction of the turning roulette wheel, and ends when the ball has come to rest on a winning number.

Players may place a variety of bets, each with different odds. A *Straight Up Bet*, for instance, may be placed on any single number, 1 through 36, and has the best odds; a *Column Bet* may be placed on any of the 12 numbers in the column; a *Dozen Bet* may be placed on a set of twelve numbers, 1-12, 13-24 or 25-36. Bets may also be placed on the color of a number—i.e. *Red* or *Black*—or on *Odd* or *Even* numbers. Additionally, a variety of combination bets can be placed—*Split*, on either of 2 numbers split; *Row*, on any of the 3 numbers in the row; *Corner*), on any of the 4 numbers forming a corner, etc.

CRAPS

Craps is perhaps as exciting a game as Roulette. It is played on a large table, with a player or "shooter" rolling a pair of dice. A variety of bets can be placed, with the outcome of each bet dependent upon the point total of the two dice when they come to rest after being rolled.

On a *Pass Line Bet*, if the first roll of dice—known as a "Come Out Roll"—has a point value of 7 or 11, the player wins. If a 2, 3 or 12 is rolled, the player loses or "craps out." If a number other than 2, 3, 12, 7 or 11 is rolled, that becomes the player's "Pass Line Point," and a player must then roll the Pass Line Point before rolling a 7 in order to win. If a 7 is rolled before the point is made, the Pass Line bet loses and the shooter "sevens out," whereupon the dice pass to the next player. A player, however, does not have to also be the shooter to place a Pass Line Bet.

The *Don't Pass Line Bet* is more or less the exact reverse of the Pass Line Bet. A 3 or 12 wins (2 is a standoff), and a 7 or 11 loses. Once a Point has been established, a 7 must be rolled before a point in order to wine, while a point thrown before a 7 automatically loses.

A *Come Bet* or *Don't Come Bet* may be placed at any time after a Pass Line Point has been established. Once a Come Bet has been placed, the same rules of winning and losing apply to it as to the Pass Line Bet. In the case of the Don't Come Bet, the same win-lose rules apply to this as to the Don't Pass Line Bet.

In addition to the Pass Line, Don't Pass Line, Come and Don't Come bets, a variety of other bets may be made—*Hardaway Betw, Horn High Bets, Field Bets, Place Bets, Buy* and *Lay Bets, Big 6* and *Big 8 Bets*, and the like—each with different odds.

KENO

Keno, quite simply, is a game of guessing numbers. Typically, in a game of Keno, 20 balls, each with a distinct number, are randomly picked from a pool of 80 balls and established as the winning numbers. The object of the game is to try to guess the winning numbers prior to the random selection of these. Players may wager various amounts, with the odds varying, depending on the number of spots guessed correctly. There are, of course, as with any other casino game, several different ways to play, with different types of bets available, and numerous ways to win.

GAMES

BLACKJACK

Blackjack, one of the most popular and interesting games in the casino, is a game of cards, in which the object is to have the total point value of the cards dealt to the player exceed the total point value of the dealer's hand without going over 21. If the player's hand goes over 21, it breaks and he automatically loses, even if the dealer's hand subsequently goes over 21; this is known as "bust." In determining the point total, each card takes its numerical face value, with the exception of the picture cards—King, Queen, Jack—which, each, counts as 10. An Ace may be counted either as 1 or 11, whichever the player choses.

Each game begins with the dealer dealing one card face down to each player and one card face up to himself. A second card is then dealt, face down, to each player and the dealer. A player may request additional cards—known as "hits"—until he is satisfied with his hand and decides to "stand." After all players have completed their hands, the dealer will draw an additional card on any point total of "soft 17"—an Ace and six—or less, and stand on a point total of "hard 17" or more. If the dealer exceeds 21 points and busts, all players with a point total of 21 or less win. If the dealer has a point total of 21 or less, he compares his hand to the point total of each player and takes all bets that are less. If a player's point count is the same as that of the dealer, it is a standoff or "push," and the dealer leaves the player's bet. In the event that a player's or dealer's initial two cards total 21—comprising an Ace and a 10, Jack, Queen or King—it is called a "Blackjack." When both the dealer and player have a Blackjack, it is a "push," with no winners.

POKER

Poker, undeniably, is America's best-known card game, in which, quite simply, the highest hand wins. Players are dealt five cards each, and wagers are made, in turn, in a clockwise rotation, beginning with the player dealt the card with the highest face value. Bets may be matched by other players, or "raised"—increased—by amounts equal to or greater than the original bet or preceding raise. A player may also elect to "fold," or give up his hand and thereby any claim to the "pot." Game rules and limits, of course, vary with each different type of game played, and it is therefore suggested that prospective players inquire from the casino's card room dealers before beginning.

In any case, Poker hands are ranked in value, from the highest hand to the lowest hand, as follows:

Royal Flush — The highest straight flush, comprising a 10, Jack, Queen, King and Ace of the same suit.
Straight Flush — Five consecutive cards in the same suit.
Four-of-a-Kind — Four cards of the same rank and value.
Full House — A combination of three-of-a-kind and a pair.
Flush — Five cards of the same suit.
Straight — Five consecutive cards, regardless of suit.
Three-of-a-Kind — Three cards of the same rank and value.
Two Pairs — Two groups of two cards of the same value.
One Pair — Two cards of the same rank and value.
High Card — The highest value card in a hand.

PINE CONES

Silver Pine

Jeffrey Pine

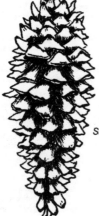

Sugar Pine

Yellow Pine

Lodgepole Pine

Foxtail Pine

Pinyon Pine

Whitebark Pine

LAKE TAHOE FISH

Lake Trout

Brook Trout

Brown Trout

Golden Trout

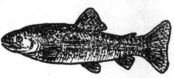

Rainbow Trout

Kokanee Salmon

Lahontan Cutthroat Trout

Mountain Whitefish

Paiute Cutthroat

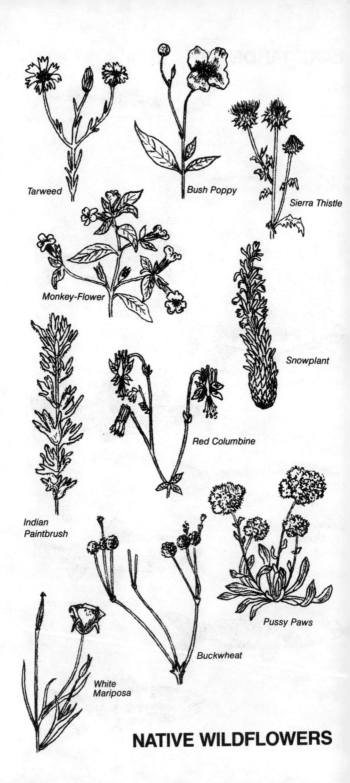

Tarweed

Bush Poppy

Sierra Thistle

Monkey-Flower

Snowplant

Red Columbine

Indian Paintbrush

Pussy Paws

White Mariposa

Buckwheat

NATIVE WILDFLOWERS

SIERRA WILDLIFE

Gray Squirrel

Ground Squirrel

Chipmunk

Muskrat

Raccoon

Beaver

Coyote

Black Bear

Gray Fox

INDEX

The abbreviation SLT stands for South Lake Tahoe
The abbreviation NLT stands for North Lake Tahoe